COMPULSIVE
EATERS
AND
RELATIONSHIPS

*Ending
the
Isolation*

COMPULSIVE EATERS AND RELATIONSHIPS

Ending the Isolation

Aphrodite Matsakis

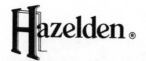

Hazelden ®

First published August, 1988.

ISBN: 0-89486-543-9
Library of Congress Catalog Card Number: 88-80895

Printed in the United States of America.

Editor's Note:
   Hazelden Educational Materials offers a variety of information on chemical dependency and related areas. Our
publications do not necessarily represent Hazelden or its
programs, nor do they officially speak for any Twelve Step
organization.
   The following publisher has generously given permission to paraphrase material from a copyrighted work:
From *Childhood and Society,* copyright 1950, by Erik H.
Erikson. Permission granted from Erik Erikson and The
Hogarth Press, London, England.

The stories of people used in this book are not based on any one person's experience but are drawn from composite experiences of many compulsive eaters.

CONTENTS

INTRODUCTION

Compulsive Eating: A Disease of Isolation

Want to get away from it all? Try compulsive eating. It's a disease of isolation. When we are practicing our illness, either by bingeing, shopping for food, or counting our calories for the tenth time, we tend to withdraw from others — friends and enemies alike. Often we may choose to be alone because we feel unattractive or bloated from a binge. Perhaps our stomachs are only sticking out an inch or two, but we think we look like a balloon. Our disease demands privacy. Simply put, most of us can't eat the way we want in front of others.

How many times have we waited impatiently for others to leave (or go to sleep) so we could indulge or purge? We may have been disagreeable or we may have encouraged others to leave us alone in other ways — so we could eat. Or we may have stolen food or money from our family members or friends to support our illness, compounding our sense of shame and guilt and leading us to more isolation and food abuse. Did the guilt from hurting or rejecting others cause us to eat more?

Perhaps we repeatedly turned down invitations so we could stay home to read, study, or work on a project. These activities were worthwhile. Yet for some of us, they were like our compulsive overeating: ways of hiding from others or escaping into a fantasy world. Or perhaps we felt compelled to overachieve at school or at work to compensate for our eating disorder or other perceived inferiorities. Yet, some of us ate continuously while reading or rewarded ourselves with our favorite binge food for working so hard. The more we ate, the more we withdrew into more and more work and more and more food.

Yet we ate out of loneliness because we believed we didn't have satisfying relationships or didn't know how to establish them. Or perhaps we were being repeatedly hurt in a relationship and didn't know how to stand up for ourselves or walk away from the relationship entirely.

1

Prior to O.A., many of us didn't know how to protect ourselves from others without eating or withdrawing. We didn't know how to have fun with others either. Since we couldn't wear our long black raincoats to the pool or to the party, we stayed home. Or perhaps we would attend only if we were sure that other overweight persons would be there. And once there, perhaps we spent more time hovering around the buffet table than socializing. Even if we didn't attack the food, we might have spent much of our emotional energy fighting the temptation. Either way, our food obsession kept us from talking with others or joining the fun.

Before we joined O.A., our "fun" came mostly from eating and food-related activities — baking, cooking, shopping for food, reading cookbooks or diet and exercise books, watching T.V. cooking shows or sporting events, collecting recipes, attending family reunions and wedding receptions, and day-dreaming about food. Yet the solitary nature of much of our food "fun" hurt our ability to share really fun activities with others.

When we first came to O.A., our focus was usually on the shape of our bodies and our harmful food habits, rather than on the health of our relationships. Often our first — and most urgent — need was to learn to eat moderately and safely. But the program taught us that long-term recovery involves more than weighing and measuring our meals and mastering other weight control techniques. It also involves developing a deep sense of self-worth. Using the Twelve Steps as a guide, we can take a close look at how we relate to ourselves and to others.

Many of us have learned through relapses that our food addiction couldn't be helped unless we stayed spiritually fit and practiced the Twelve Steps to the best of our ability in all our affairs. Frightened by the prospect of dealing with our disappointments and relationship conflicts, we're often tempted to return to the sedation of excess food. Yet our daily challenge is to learn to live with ourselves and others, one day at a time, without panicking, without turning to compulsive eating for comfort, and without making other self-destructive choices.

2

PART 1

Why Relationships Can Be Difficult For Compulsive Eaters

Common Obstacles to Healthy Relationships

Many compulsive eaters have difficulty coping with change. We tend to have a strong need for constancy and certainty in our lives. Many times we find ourselves unwilling to give up control over people and events. Our relationships with others present one of our greatest challenges: accepting and adapting to change. We may often feel more comfortable with food, an inert substance that never changes, rather than with people, who are constantly changing.

For example, we may see someone changing and think he or she is abandoning us. In some cases the person may truly be growing away from us. In other cases, however, that person is growing as an individual, and is not necessarily rejecting us. Yet we may mistakenly assume that we're no longer wanted or needed.

"Before O.A., I couldn't handle anyone's changing," explains Janice. "It was too much for me, even if their change was positive. Now I'm getting my head out of the refrigerator — and the toilet bowl — and accepting the fact that, as much as I don't like it, everyone can't stand still just for me."

Janice is also coming to realize how much others have been afraid to tell her of their changing feelings. While she is annoyed at being "treated like a child," she realizes that her anxiety over change hasn't been as well-hidden as she had thought. "I'm the one who taught everybody to be so protective of me," she says.

Janice wants her family and friends to know that she will not fall apart or binge-out if change is imminent or necessary.

Emotions On Hold

During our years of food abuse, our emotional development was put on the shelf. Many of us were not able to participate fully in relationships.

"I'm thirteen," states Sheila, 40. Like many O.A. members, Sheila frankly admits that when she began to compulsively overeat, she stopped growing emotionally. At thirteen, she used food to solve her relationship problems. But, of course, the food solved nothing. She can now see how some of her adolescent relationship conflicts keep her from maintaining satisfying work and love relationships. She is working to resolve these conflicts by expressing her feelings and needs.

Many of us are experts at losing weight. Perhaps we've lost excess pounds several times, either through O.A. or with the help of a commercial diet club. But unless we address the emotional issues underlying our compulsion, we'll probably revert back to food when we have relationship problems we're not prepared to handle.

Often our present difficulties in relating to others stem in part from arrested development at one of the eight stages of development. Erik Erikson, author of *Childhood and Society*, the first book to look at the developmental stages of the human personality across the entire lifespan, identified these eight stages: (1) trust vs. mistrust; (2) autonomy vs. shame and doubt; (3) initiative vs. guilt; (4) industry vs. inferiority; (5) identity vs. role confusion; (6) intimacy vs. isolation; (7) growth vs. stagnation; and (8) ego integrity vs. despair.

In the first stage, the issue we face is that of trust vs. mistrust. As an infant, we learned either to trust or not trust that our caretaker would provide for us and be there for us. If our experience taught us that our caretaker would be predictable and constant, we learned to trust others as well as ourselves. If, on the other hand, our caretakers were faulty, we may have started turning to excess food in hopes of finding the care we missed. Or we may find ourselves attracted to people who cook for us or to gatherings where there is food.

If our caretakers were untrustworthy, we may have learned to put our trust in the one predictable item they would usually provide for us: food. "There was no love in my home, only food," explains John, whose mother physically abused him. Therefore, at an early age, John learned to put his trust in food rather than in others. In O.A., however, he began to learn to turn to other O.A. members or a Higher Power in times of need. He realized that food had no real power to care for him.

Due to such early experiences, John still has some difficulty trusting others. On some level, he still expects that others will be like his mother: neglectful and abusive. If we, like John, suffered from emotional or physical abuse as children, we may also mistrust others.

Some of us, like John, learned to blame ourselves for our caretakers' inattention or inconsistencies. Years later, if we're in a relationship where someone betrays us, we may return to our original childhood feelings: we think we're being neglected, treated inconsistently, or abused because of some defect on our part. We then use food as a way of punishing ourselves for our perceived inadequacies.

Turning to food, however, keeps us in the childlike attitude of self-blame and fear. It prevents us from realistically assessing our relationships. In addition, food abuse keeps us mistrusting ourselves, making it more difficult for us to learn to trust that others or a Higher Power will care for us in a consistent, loving, and not punishing manner.

In the second stage, that of autonomy vs. shame and doubt, children struggle to be free and to express themselves without making parents or other adults angry. If we, as children, weren't carefully guided in learning to make free choices, we may still have difficulty being independent. Or, if our first attempts to be independent met with failure or with disapproval from others, we may still associate independence with

6

shame and self-doubt. The slightest hint of disapproval from others may compel us to change our plans or goals.

Overcoming our fears and the restrictions of others to reach our potential are issues we also face in the third stage (initiative vs. guilt) and in the fourth stage (industry vs. inferiority). When, as adults, we abuse food, we stay stuck at these early stages. We're afraid to act, lest we fail and feel ashamed, guilty, and inferior. Yet we also eat because we're ashamed of our inability to act independently, show initiative, or be productive.

The fifth stage, that of identity vs. role confusion, usually coincides with puberty. Many of us began our food abuse during this stage of life and never finished defining our relationships to our peers, our parents, and other adults.

Our lack of self-definition may have kept us from forming intimate relationships with others. This is the task we confront during the sixth stage, that of intimacy vs. isolation. While we were busy buying food, preparing it, bingeing or starving, and hating ourselves for it, others were busy taking risks in relationships, making mistakes, and learning from them. In contrast, many of us fearfully hid behind compulsive eating.

For some of us, the preoccupation with food began a vicious cycle. Because we tended to interact less with others, we didn't develop social skills. On those occasions when we did try to mix with others, we felt awkward and vulnerable, which may have led us to withdraw even further. Once alone, however, we were deprived of the stimulation and comfort of human companionship, and often turned to food out of loneliness.

In our middle and later years, the tasks before us are those of stage seven (growth vs. stagnation) and stage eight (ego integrity vs. despair). As we approach these years of our life, we more than ever need to feel that our life has meaning and purpose. If we're to avoid stagnation and despair, we need to reach out to others. And we need to look within, rather than to others, for approval and direction. If we turn to food, we will once again isolate ourselves and suffer physically, emotionally, intellectually, and spiritually. This deprives others of our gifts.

The O.A. program of recovery provides us with meetings, sponsors, and friends. With these resources we can discuss our problems and try to resolve them, one day at a time.

Emotions

Many of us tend to be emotionally intense and suffer from mood swings. Both can create significant problems in relationships. "Lighten up" is an often-heard, much-needed slogan for those of us in O.A. who tend to take life, ourselves, and others too seriously.

"I love hard, hate hard, work hard, and play hard," says Barbara, an O.A. member. She gets anxious over comments friends or co-workers make. Her husband and daughter feel that she overreacts to most problems and interactions with people. "Taking everything personally is part of my script," Barbara explains.

We often spend much of our energy defending ourselves against other people, as opposed to participating actively in relationships. We find it hard to relax. It's easy to see why we turn to eating to reduce tension!

When we change our relationships with food, we lose our buffer. Barbara, for example, has difficulty handling her emotions. When she doesn't use food to stabilize herself emotionally, she's left feeling her true emotions. This often seems overwhelming to her. While Barbara's ability to feel deeply is one of her strengths, when she suffers over minor events in her relationships, it can seem more like a curse than a blessing.

Barbara tries but can't hide the intensity of her feelings from her husband. She is even less able to conceal her mood swings. Sometimes Barbara seesaws from "high" to "low" several times a day. Sometimes these mood swings happen when she deviates from her food plan. But they also occur when she is abstinent.

Because her husband and some friends are not compulsive eaters and appear more emotionally stable than herself, Barbara often feels inferior to them. In conversations, she is often defensive and apologizes for herself. She's angry at herself for not having more self-esteem, but doesn't know how to obtain it. Consequently, she sometimes withdraws from these relationships. Or she may be present in body only, creating relationship difficulties.

Barbara's problem is compounded by a fairly common American attitude that to be highly emotional is considered a sign of weakness or mental instability. If we're too happy, too sad, too angry, or too enthusiastic, others may judge us as neurotic or abnormal.

In recovery, we should expect to feel more emotional. "Is this what normal people — who don't compulsively eat — feel like?" asks Barbara. She's referring to the fear, anxiety, and pain she often feels when confronting someone on a difficult issue.

When Barbara stopped compulsively eating and started facing her feelings, she began to judge herself as "crazy," "emotionally deficient," and even "insane." Because her feelings were intense, and often painful, she felt she wasn't in recovery. She expected that abstinence and following the Twelve Steps would result in constant emotional peace. She learned, however, that strong feelings are part of recovery — and life — not signs of insanity.

Impulsive Behavior

Some of us have trouble controlling our impulses, not only with food, but in the way we express our feelings. Some of us, in an attempt to be open, blurt out our feelings on the spot, without thinking how we might be affecting others. Then, regretting our hasty remarks, we suffer guilt and remorse. This behavior can set us up for a binge or some other form of self-punishment.

Our first challenge as recovering compulsive eaters is to become aware of our feelings for others rather than stuffing down these feelings with food. The second challenge is accepting our feelings, all of them, and not punishing ourselves if we have some negative ones. Our third challenge is deciding what to do with them — taking action. Just as we have the choice of eating or remaining abstinent, we also have the choice of how, when, and if to express our emotions or thoughts to another person.

In O.A. we learn to forgive ourselves for inappropriate outbursts. We also learn that we can think before we act. Just as we don't have to eat everything in front of us or run for the refrigerator whenever we have a food thought, we don't have to automatically respond to every person and event in our life. One O.A. member explains, "Sometimes the most important thing I do for myself is stay quiet."

Even if we're asked to share our thoughts or feelings, we don't have to do so automatically. All we have to do with our feelings, at any particular moment, is to acknowledge them. We don't have to react in some impulsive manner we may regret later. Nor do we have to give in if another person insists that we tell all about ourselves. Eventually, we may choose to share our feelings. We can give ourselves time to think about which feelings we want to share and which ones are best kept to ourselves. Also, we can ask our O.A. friends for help in expressing ourselves clearly, honestly, and effectively.

Family Backgrounds and Abuse

We can't blame all of our problems on a dysfunctional family background. But if we've come from a dysfunctional family, we've probably learned unhealthy patterns of relating to others. Abstinence alone will not teach us how to relate to others in healthy, self-respecting ways. We must examine the relationship patterns of our dysfunctional families, deal with the feelings associated with those patterns, and then go on to practice new and better ways of relating to others.

Perhaps as children we were given double messages — for example, "Grow up, but don't grow up." Or perhaps we were rejected, but the rejection was lied about. Often, children who were overtly rejected by their parents are less despairing than children from homes where the rejection was masked with false love — or with food. When the rejection was plainly stated, the child could go on to make new friends outside the family. But when the rejection was hidden, or subtle, the child was bound to the family in this state of confusion. He or she may have tried hard to gain love and approval, but frequently failed to do so, not due to any inadequacy, but because of unhealthy family relationships.

As children some of us suffered emotional or physical abuse or suffered from growing up with alcoholic parents. As adults we may have to face considerable pain and gain insight before we can interact with people, free of the negative patterns of our past.

Special problems arise for those of us who came from dysfunctional families and who are now working in dysfunctional environments. We may find ourselves reenacting old roles of "victim" or "saviour." Professional help, as well as additional O.A. meetings and making phone calls to friends for support, may be needed to help us separate the past from the present.

A common pattern for some of us is to take responsibility for a bad workplace or to emotionally overreact to events

12

there. We may then return home drained, both emotionally and physically, yet still feeling guilty because of work left undone or tensions left unresolved. In such a state, it's easy to turn to food.

Histories of Physical or Sexual Abuse

"Lots of times when I cry in O.A. meetings, it's not me crying, but her," says Phyllis. "I'm a full grown woman, who functions well and is responsible and mature (except sometimes with food). But inside me is a crippled little girl. She's ugly and battered, with a bloody nose, black eyes, and a busted lip, and aches and pains all over from where she was kicked. But she's me and until I realized that she was me, I had no peace and could not become abstinent."

Many mental health professionals believe childhood physical and sexual abuse, as well as rape and battering as an adult, can lead the victim to developing a substance abuse problem. These traumas are of such magnitude, horror, or duration that they overwhelm the person's emotional and physical coping strengths. When someone we love abuses us, it is the ultimate betrayal. For a child there's probably nothing more painful than being verbally, physically, or sexually abused by a parent — the very person whose love, protection, and care the child so desperately needs. Similarly, it can be devastating for a woman when a man responds to her love with hate and violence.

According to psychoanalyst Sarah Haley, trauma emerges when a person is made into an object. Whether one's assailant is a tornado, an angry mother, an incestuous father, or a violent husband, at the moment of attack the victim doesn't feel like a human being with the right to safety, happiness, and health. At that moment, the victim almost becomes a thing, a vulnerable object subject to the will of a malignant power. When the assailant is a natural force, such as an earthquake, the catastrophe can be explained away as an "accident of fate."

But when the assailant is another person, especially one who is close to the victim, the victim's trust in other people, in a Higher Power, and in society can be severely shaken.

During the traumatic event, the victim may shut down emotionally in order to survive the event. Long after the event the victim may continue to numb awareness of the trauma with the use of alcohol and other drugs or food. Recent research shows that victims of abuse may use one or more substances to block out their recollection of the trauma and the associated feelings of powerlessness, depersonalization, grief, and anger.

For some of us who have been through trauma, food has numbed our awareness of the event; when we enter O.A. we have only a dim memory of the past. Only when we gain some degree of physical and emotional recovery do we begin to remember the painful details. Phyllis, for example, didn't begin to deal with having been physically and sexually abused as a child until her third year of recovery. Although she hadn't forgotten her experiences, she dismissed them as unimportant and irrelevant to her present life. When she took another Fourth Step review, Phyllis realized she had glossed over some of her childhood experiences, preferring to minimize their horror and their impact on her. "I'm scared," she told her sponsor. "Scared that if I begin to deal with the abuse, I'll start to eat and gain back all the weight. Scared, too, that if I don't deal with it, I might start eating." Phyllis also feared that if she examined her past, she might no longer want or need her husband, who she married mainly to escape a violent home.

Phyllis wanted to share her story at O.A. meetings but felt she couldn't. What if she sounded like she was "on the pity pot," lacking an "attitude of gratitude," or "making excuses" for her illness? Worse yet, what if nobody believed her or thought she was asking for sympathy?

With the help of a well-informed sponsor and therapist Phyllis came to appreciate that there was "healing in the telling." She realized that as a trauma victim she needed healing no matter what the consequences would be.

Those of us who have been physically or emotionally abused ate (or starved ourselves) to block out the bitter pain. Yet no amount of food or dieting could save us from the pain. We often recall our psychological hurts more than our physical ones. For example, John reports that he still bears scars on his chest from the hot iron his mother used to brand him with as a punishment. "But the brand on my heart from being told I was a no-good son and an unwanted child are far more real to me. At 47, I'm still not over it," he says.

"I can almost forget the rapes," another O.A. member states. "But in my mind I still hear my father calling me a 'bad girl' for letting him touch me, for having sexual parts, for not making him happy."

As much as we've tried to forget the past, we may find ourselves suffering from one or more of the various long-term effects of trauma: depression, fear of others, and hypersensitivity to criticism and rejection.

Blaming Ourselves

We may tend to blame ourselves for our victimization. Even if we have been told by a caring friend, an O.A. member, or a therapist that being beaten or sexually molested by a family member wasn't our fault, we may still not be able to ease the voice inside that holds us responsible. We weren't born with this accusatory voice. Rather it was put there, in large part, by our abuser.

We may carry this self-accusing attitude into our relationships today, taking responsibility for a relationship problem and focusing on our shortcomings (real or imagined).

We tend to forget how, when we were abused, we felt trapped, and our abuser threatened to harm us or another person if we told or ran away.

15

Rather than be trampled on again, we often withdraw from others or enter or maintain relationships at a certain emotional distance. But at the same time we desire to trust and lean on another person. We may accept or remain in relationships that don't satisfy us, feeling we have no choice and should be grateful to receive attention from anyone.

We may also alienate ourselves from others because we fear our potential for violence. Even though we may have hated our abusers, we may also have secretly admired their power and learned how to imitate them. In anger we may lash out at our children or other loved ones.

Often, we take out our anger in overeating, spending, or other compulsive behaviors. Until we uncover and deal with the trauma, our present relationships will suffer.

The healing process can be painful and difficult, but with professional help and the support of the O.A. program we can learn to stop blaming ourselves.

According to some therapists, persons with eating disorders often suffer abandonment anxiety: a strong fear of being deserted by others. We may have developed eating disorders as defenses against the hurt and sadness we felt from being disregarded or unloved. Rather than feeling the hurt — and the anger — we ate.

Our fear of being deserted may profoundly affect our relationships, both at home and at work. We may avoid having relationships, or limit them severely, not only because we are ashamed of our bodies, but also because we fear rejection.

For those of us who were overweight, we could always blame our relationship problems on our fat. But when the fat is no longer good for an excuse, we must confront the possibility of being rejected for some aspect of our personality, or one of our values. This can hurt us even more than being rejected for our size or shape. Until we gain a sufficient level of self-acceptance, we may not have the inner strength to risk the inevitable pains involved in human relationships.

Working the program requires that we know our character defects. Certain personality traits common to many compulsive eaters can interfere with relationships. These are some common ones: impatience, frustration, low tolerance level, anger, depression, procrastination, fear, and dishonesty. We may also compulsively work, spend, or exercise. While it may be healthier for us to throw ourselves into our work or into the local swimming pool than retreat to the refrigerator, if we're constantly working or exercising we are less available for others.

We need to examine our motives: Are we working longer hours or exercising more because we're running from or avoiding certain relationships? Are we perhaps expecting too much from others, as we do of ourselves? Does our exercise or work schedule control us, or are we in control? Can we let go of our routine when someone needs us, or are we inflexible, making our exercise or work plans more important than the people in our lives?

In recovery, we learn to curb our compulsiveness and to become more honest, patient, and caring. Our previous suffering helps us have more compassion for others who are hurting or in emotional need.

17

Accepting the Good

We may compulsively eat due to rejection and other hurts in our relationships, but we may also eat due to success in forming positive, healthy relationships. Perhaps we don't feel worthy of a loving relationship, or we're unable to accept the good in relationships. Regardless of how much weight we've lost or how much we've yet to lose, until we learn to love ourselves, we may have difficulty receiving love or respect from others.

"I carry around my own black cloud," explains Susan, who called herself "Ms. Angry and Negative" until she joined O.A. There she learned to try to see her cup as half full rather than half empty. Although Susan is at goal weight, she still feels she doesn't deserve her present boyfriend, who she describes as "wonderful." Susan looks with envy and admiration upon Lisa, an O.A. member with many more pounds to lose, but who has learned to value herself and to consider herself deserving of a loving relationship.

Some of us feel we don't even deserve O.A. Sometimes we find ourselves eating after meetings because we can't accept the support of other members. Or we have difficulty accepting the peace that can come from working the Steps.

Susan, for example, is still trying to learn how to live without imagining or creating crises in her relationships. Having lived with crises for so long, she has become almost accustomed to feeling tormented or obsessed about one relationship or another, especially her relationship with her boyfriend. Some of her anxieties may stem from having lived in an alcoholic home. But many of these anxieties were — and are — generated by her out-of-control eating that causes her to feel insecure. Now that she's aware of her tendency to anticipate problems with others that do not yet exist, Susan asks herself in her morning meditation, "Is there a thorn in some particular relationship today? If so, did I put it there?

Can I take it away? Do I really need to get hysterical or can I make a phone call or do some writing instead?"

Each of us can make efforts every day to appreciate the good in our lives. Through prayer, meditation, and meetings we can chase away our black cloud.

PART 2

Common Relationship Dynamics

Overdependence On Others

While some compulsive eaters are socially outgoing and full of self-confidence, many of us know self-doubt, low self-esteem, and social isolation all too well. "When I was five years old, someone told me I had a big nose and fat legs," says Paula. "For the next 30 years, that's how I saw myself. O.A. has shown me my positive features such as intelligence and sparkling blue eyes. But I still have trouble feeling good about myself."

Despite O.A. teaching us that we are powerless over our disease, we may still feel there is something wrong with us. We may mistrust ourselves and overlook our positive characteristics. Others (especially thin persons or normal eaters) might appear "better" than us. We might try to emulate them, or try hard to please them, rather than develop our own potential and learn how to please ourselves. We may also become vulnerable to the opinions of others and follow their directions rather than our own instincts.

According to the *Twelve Steps and Twelve Traditions:*

> Our egomania digs two disastrous pitfalls. Either we insist upon dominating the people we know, or, we depend upon them far too much. If we lean too heavily on people, they will sooner or later fail us, for they are human too, and cannot possibly meet our incessant demands. In this way our insecurity grows and festers. When we habitually try to manipulate others to our own willful desires, they revolt, and resist us heavily. Then we develop hurt feelings, a sense of persecution, and a desire to retaliate. As we redouble our efforts at control, and continue to fail, our suffering becomes acute and constant.

We often have relationship difficulties because we depend too much on others. Or we may try to control them. Yet, emotional growth requires that we develop the ability to evaluate and make our own values and goals rather than to let others impose them on us. In recovery, we gain the ability to let go of others, to detach not only from their problems and their pain but from their reactions to us.

As painful as it is, we slowly learn that just as we are powerless over food, we are powerless over people. While we can think about and control our actions toward others, we can't control their reactions to us. The more energy we use worrying about the reactions of others, the less we have to consider our needs and pursue our goals.

In O.A., we learn to depend on the Twelve Steps rather than on any specific individual. Sometimes following the Steps may create conflicts with others; they may not understand why, or how, we are changing. Many misunderstandings, however, can be overcome with clear and loving communication. When such communication doesn't reduce tensions, we may need to reevaluate the relationship.

Emotional Security: The "Magic Rescuer"

For many of us, relationships, especially intimate ones, are characterized by the search for emotional security. *If only someone would love me, I could love myself* is a common feeling. Perhaps we hope that another person — whether it be our sponsor, our spouse, or some other individual — will "rescue" us, not only from our low self-esteem, but from our pain, confusion, and grief.

Jane hoped that by having a boyfriend she wouldn't have to deal with the pain and reality of her mother's alcoholism. Sarah, on the other hand, was looking for a special relationship that would rescue her from food compulsion. Veronica married a strong, dominating man in hopes that he would help her control her bingeing. He managed to help her control her eating, but he also managed to control almost everything else about her, including her activities at work, her social relationships, even the way she parented their children. Eventually, he became physically abusive. But Veronica was afraid to leave him because she depended on him to help her with her food compulsion. Despite his help she found herself bingeing or spending hours preoccupied with food.

As most long-term O.A. members know, neither sex nor the love and strength of another person can deliver us from dealing with our disease, with our past, or with our present problems at home or work. We can't put the responsibility for our lives on another person. The search for a "magic rescuer" who will meet all our needs and save us from ourselves is but another version of the "geographical cure." Erich Fromm, one of the first therapists to describe the human struggle against social and personal pressures to conform, calls it an escape from freedom. If we look to a partner, friend, or sponsor to take over our life, it will be restricted by narrow borders and we may never develop healthy self-reliance.

How much we are dependent on a magic rescuer will determine our self-reliance to stand alone. If we expect to get everything we want in life from another person, we will not be forced to extend ourselves and struggle for what we want, intellectually or emotionally. Our dependency doesn't eliminate feelings of helplessness and insecurity; it only perpetuates them. Further, if we're dependent on a magic rescuer, we may find ourselves spending much of our energy figuring how to please the other person so as not to lose him or her. Or, rather than take responsibility for our own lives, we might manipulate our rescuers so they will continue to guide, protect, and strengthen us.

As much as we need and desire these people, we may also resent our dependency on them. We may find ourselves rebelling against them or having hostile feelings toward them. Since we might think it's dangerous to be angry at people we need so much, we may hide or repress our feelings. This creates yet another internal conflict for us, which we may try to resolve by excess eating.

Excess eating, however, only perpetuates our dependency on others. When we practice our old eating habits, our self-esteem diminishes and we may need to turn to others to help us feel worthy and attractive. As we learn to believe in a Power greater than ourselves and turn our will and our lives over to its care, we gain more faith in ourselves. Working the Twelve Steps helps restore balance in our relationships.

Abstinence

Because we fear the reawakening of the food obsession, many of us adopt the slogan, "Abstinence is the most important thing in my life without exception." Only as we attempt to live with this slogan do we realize that abstinence involves much more than eliminating certain foods or certain quantities of foods. For many of us, abstinence leads to a new way of living, to new relationships, or to significant changes in our relationships.

Abstinence is the basis of our emotional and spiritual growth, the lifelong processes that must be embraced with courage and honesty if we're to stay in recovery. Although O.A. doesn't furnish food plans, it suggests seeing qualified professionals regarding nutrition or food planning. Abstinence is a highly individual matter. Some of us have three meals a day with nothing in between except noncaloric liquids. Others include one or more planned snacks. While some of us eliminate sugar and white flour from our diets, some of us do include small portions of these with no ill effects.

By working the Steps, we have found emotional balance, spiritual joy, and happiness. But sloppy abstinence, bingeing, or other dips into food make it more difficult for us to listen to ourselves, to others, or to our Higher Power. Extra bites eventually result not only in excess pounds but in increased cravings and increased food thoughts. Both can be painful and debilitating.

Breaking abstinence or otherwise being compulsive about food can also lead to a flare up of our character defects. It can fan the fires of certain self-destructive behaviors that typically lead to even more compulsive eating.

"A binge is a binge," says John. "Whether it's a pound of cheese or a pound of candy, it's still compulsive eating." Since cheese triggers his compulsion, John has found that he must abstain from it, as well as from certain other foods.

John's wife, however, loves cheese. In fact, John met her at a wine and cheese party. Before O.A., much of their social life revolved around events that involved food. When John decided to make his abstinence a priority and asked his wife to help him by removing all cheese from the home, she was annoyed.

"You mean I can't even have a cheese sandwich anymore?" she asked. "Just because you have an eating disorder, why should I suffer?"

While John's wife was upset about not being able to have one of her favorite foods in the home, on a deeper level, she also felt rejected. It seemed as if John wasn't just abstaining from a certain food but also from an important part of their relationship.

John, too, felt unloved. Yet his wife did love him, just like our family members may love us. They may strongly desire to support our recovery. But we must expect such friction when we ask that our binge foods be removed from the home or assert our need to eat at certain times.

"Why can't you be normal and eat with us like you used to?" or "What are you not eating now?" we might be asked. At such times, we may feel belittled, or we might become angry. Why can't our loved ones and friends understand how precious abstinence is to us? Can't they see how hard it has been for us to become willing to be abstinent? Shouldn't they be admiring our desire to go to these lengths?

At this point, some of us might stay away from the family dinner table or from other eating occasions. In doing so, we may manage to preserve our abstinence. But if we want to preserve our family ties and friendships also, we need to find new and meaningful ways of relating. This can present quite a challenge since, throughout the centuries, the sharing of food has been central to family life and to certain religious and social gatherings. At all levels of relationships eating with another person symbolizes friendship, commitment, or some values and common purpose.

When we stay away from the table or insist on eating a special diet, we may be perceived not only as different but as somehow disloyal. Our need to stay abstinent can be easily misinterpreted as aloofness or distancing ourselves from others.

We may feel the pain of being separate when we don't eat as others do. Consequently, we're tempted to deviate from our food plan and join them. But if we're committed to abstinence, we can't feel that we belong by eating like everyone else. Some foods may be like poison for us, and some eating times may be disastrous for us.

Prior to O.A., many of us were erratic not only about what we ate but when we ate. We ate at different times on different days, depending on our mood, our latest diet, our latest binge, or the weather. Many of us were on relentless "diet-binge" cycles where we starved ourselves during certain hours or certain days only to indulge later. In O.A. we learn the importance of feeding our bodies on a regular schedule. We can't afford to become too hungry or too tired. Maintaining our abstinence may require not only more regular meals but a more regular sleep schedule. Both can deeply affect our relationships, especially our intimate ones.

Before O.A., John used to skip breakfast, have a mini-lunch, then eat almost nonstop from dinner to bedtime. More than half his calories were consumed after ten, when he and his wife would discuss their day over snacks. John's wife ate a moderate amount; John would eat everything left on the platter, then go to the kitchen for more.

The next morning John would need at least five cups of coffee to overcome the sedating effects of his late night binge. The coffee, however, gave him a false sense of energy, leading him to believe that he didn't need to eat again until the evening. By dinnertime, he was ravenous and pounced on the food like a wolf.

In O.A. John found that having a moderate breakfast and a lunch helped control his evening binges. Whenever he could bypass the 10:00 P.M. snack routine with his wife, the next day he would wake up fresh and alert and not need his usual five or six cups of coffee.

John's abstinence improved both his outlook on life and his work performance. But it didn't improve his marriage. When his wife pulled out the snacks at 10:00 P.M. and John would not join in, sometimes she was angry. After all, she had spent hours preparing his favorite treats as a sign of her love for him. Why was he now, after all these years, abandoning their evening ritual? Couldn't he have just one? Surely one bite wouldn't hurt.

"One bite is too many and a thousand bites is not enough!" John roared, chasing his wife out of the room. What was she trying to do, sabotage his recovery?

True, John was angry at his wife for continually offering him snacks even though she knew he had a disease. But the intensity of his anger stemmed, in part, from his jealousy that she could eat certain snacks and he couldn't. John eventually realized that his wife wasn't being malicious but was merely a creature of habit as he was.

On a deeper level, John realized it was easier for him to talk about food and to eat with his wife than to be truly intimate with her. Instead of eating he could ask about her feelings and concerns and share his. He found that talk about his anxieties rather than the flavor and cost of foods was new and different. It also required effort, thought, and concentration. But in exchange for the snacks and the food talk, John learned to communicate with his wife.

John and his wife were lucky. Even after removing food from the center of their relationship, they still had much in common. For a while John was worried. Because his sex life was so intermingled with eating afterward, he wondered if his enthusiasm for sex was truly a desire for sex, or rather, a desire for the food that followed. After completing a Fourth Step on his sexuality, John realized that eating before or after sex had always played an important role in the excitement. But even without food, his passion for his wife remained.

Over time, John's wife came to accept her husband's addiction. When he felt shaky about his abstinence, she would have snacks by herself in another room. As John grew stronger in the program and felt less rigid about his food plan, he was able to plan a small, pre-bedtime snack for himself to eat with his wife. As his spiritual program grew, he was able to watch his wife eat her foods without becoming anxious. He couldn't, however, handle wine and cheese parties, which meant less contact with certain friends. But John's wife was willing to give up her wine and cheese parties and participate in new, food-free activities with him. Food was no longer the focus of the relationship.

Good-bye to Eating Friends

But not all of us are so fortunate. Our family members or friends may not be willing, or able, to change their food habits. Perhaps one or more of them are compulsive eaters, too, but are not in a recovery program or seeking help. We may care about these people, but we realize that our recovery comes first. In some cases, the price we pay for abstinence is not seeing some people so often, or not seeing some people at all.

Some of us have to say good-bye to our old eating friends. We do our best to explain why we need to go for a walk instead of having a heavy lunch. When friends insist we join them at the all-you-can-eat places, we tell them that we aren't rejecting them, but the excess food. Yet they might feel hurt. Some even feel we are acting superior. Others can't give up their favorite pastime to join us in a new, nonfood venture. When we stop going to lunch and dinner with them, they might stop calling us. Our invitations to movies or talks over tea might not seem like "enough" for them. If we no longer want to eat, they may no longer want to see us.

Eventually some of these relationships die a natural but not painless death. In the midst of celebrating our recovery, we are also mourning the loss of certain relationships. We might also mourn our powerlessness to save our eating friends from their possible food addiction. If we're the family chef or have a reputation for being a fabulous cook, and then we reduce our culinary pursuits for abstinence, we might feel a loss of identity. We now have to find new sources of raising our self-esteem. If we've been using our home-baked delights as gifts, we now have to find new ways of showing our love and appreciation.

As we grow in abstinence, we'll also grow in self-love and self-acceptance, and in our ability to love and accept others.

Loneliness

We often complain of feeling empty inside. This dreaded empty feeling can occur whether we're satiated with food or abstinent. It may mean we feel spiritually empty. Or it may be a defense we use against uncomfortable emotions, such as grief or pain. Or perhaps it's just normal human loneliness.

Loneliness can mean we are physically without others. Yet when we say we're lonely we often don't mean that. Instead, we feel unlistened to, unloved, or unappreciated by the people in our lives. This form of loneliness can be felt even when we're surrounded by others.

O.A. members who are single sometimes complain of the loneliness of not having a spouse or a partner. Some married O.A. members speak of loneliness too. Either their spouses are not available to them as often as they would like, or their spouses have a limited capacity for, or interest in, emotional intimacy. "I got married so I wouldn't feel lonely, but I'm lonely anyway," an O.A. member says. When her husband ignores her, she suffers and wants to eat.

Whether we're married or single, when we feel alone, the emptiness can make us anxious and may propel us to "fill up" on something. If we've given up compulsive eating, then we may try to fill up the hole inside with other people. Frantic when alone or feeling alone, we may grab for other people as we once did for food. In some cases, the obsession with food is replaced with an obsession over a relationship.

Sometimes the pain of feeling empty inside is so great we become involved in friendships or intimate relationships that hurt us. As we grow in the O.A. program, we gain the courage to break away from persons who are inhibiting our growth or abusing us. We also learn how to be alone with ourselves and not be afraid.

An O.A. member explains: "I have lots of friends, but I still get lonely. My first reaction is to panic, head for the kitchen, or call somebody, anybody, even someone I don't really want to talk to. But now I'm learning to say to myself, *There's no catastrophe going on except the one inside my head. It's only loneliness I'm feeling. Sure it hurts, but that's okay. Loneliness is a part of life and I don't have to eat over it.*

Then I ask myself, *Am I really lonely or am I just procrastinating about doing something I have to do or about making some sticky decision? Do I really need to visit a friend or run to an O.A. meeting, or do I need to sit down, listen to myself, and face some emotion, life problem, or relationship problem I've been running from?*

We may even find ourselves choosing to be alone. In the past, our choice to be alone might have represented a flight into a fantasy, a denial of our dependency needs, or an unhealthy withdrawal. In recovery, many of us find that solitude provides a much needed respite from others' demands. Solitude offers time to reflect, to get to know ourselves and our Higher Power, to make new goals, work the Steps, or find new interests.

Being Yourself

We have not once sought to be one in a family, to be a friend among friends, to be a worker among workers, to be a useful member of society. Always we tried to struggle to the top of the heap, or to hide underneath it. This self-centered behavior blocked a partnership relation with any one of those about us. Of true brotherhood, we had small comprehension.

— The Twelve Steps and Twelve Traditions

As compulsive eaters, we can suffer not only from low self-esteem, but from grandiosity, pride, and perfectionism. We may have difficulty fitting in at work or in social groups. We may not participate in a sport, for example, or volunteer for a work assignment, unless we're certain that we'll be the best.

We tend to see ourselves in extreme terms, as either all good or all bad, and often have difficulty being "ordinary" at any activity. If we're still overweight, we may withdraw for fear of being singled out as the "fatty" especially if we've been ridiculed in the past.

Losing weight, however, doesn't solve the problem of feeling uncomfortable in a group. We need to learn certain social skills, develop self-love, and risk being imperfect or ordinary in front of others. Completing Steps Four and Five often helps us see ourselves realistically.

Being Different and Unique

Sometimes we so desperately want to fit in that we fail to develop our uniqueness and individuality. Because we've been "different" for so long in being overweight or obsessed with food, we may be reluctant to reveal to others that we *are* different.

If we cease to be ourselves and mold our personality to be entirely as others would have us, we may no longer suffer from feeling alone or the anxiety of being "different." But the price we pay is the loss of self.

It hurts to be left out and seen as different. But the price of denying our identity and potential is great. In O.A. we slowly gain the courage to be ourselves. We also learn to accept that not everybody will approve of us. Our major goal is to learn to like and approve of ourselves. As one O.A. member says, "What others think of me is none of my business."

Overcoming Sex Role Stereotypes

In traditional sex roles, women are expected to express needs, warmth, self-doubt, sadness, and other emotions. In relationships they're expected to be dependent, responsible, obedient, sensitive, and to suppress their sexual and aggressive impulses. In contrast, the "real man" is expected to be a risk-taking leader who successfully manipulates the environment and is competent and creative. In relationships, the "real man" is expected to be competitive, assertive, dominant, and tough. He isn't plagued by self-doubts and doesn't express warm or tender feelings.

These traditional sex role stereotypes are impossible to live up to. Further, rigid sex role standards deny both sexes their full humanity.

In recent years, these traditional sex role stereotypes have been challenged by the women's liberation movement. There is now greater societal permission for women to display "masculine traits" and for men to reveal their "feminine" ones. But sex role stereotypes die hard, and many compulsive eaters are still struggling to define their sex roles. Some women binge to suppress their supposedly "masculine" traits; some men punish themselves with food for having "feminine" traits.

If part of having relationships includes loving and sharing with others, judging ourselves or others by traditional sex role standards is destructive. As part of recovery, many compulsive eaters learn to examine the early sex role messages they received about how a man or a woman "should" be. They learn to see their own unique personalities and the new opportunities open for both men and women at work and in relationships. Many of us can stop bingeing when we redefine our early notions of "masculinity" and "femininity."

But our bingeing hasn't ceased quickly or without struggle. Despite the progress made by the women's movement, some women still find their families or social groups reluctant to accept a "liberated woman." In some cases, the woman herself

36

isn't ready to change. Many men, meanwhile, have difficulty balancing their career and home lives.

For some women in O.A., it has been a monumental achievement to (a) recognize that they have ambitions outside of the family, and (b) take steps toward achieving those ambitions. The decision to pursue goals outside of the home has often given them guilt, interpersonal tensions, and fatigue, any one of which can lead to bingeing.

Joanne's Story

Some O.A. members report that their husbands protest when they spend as much as a half hour on themselves. "It was 'okay' for me to read women's magazines and learn how to cook and be attractive," says Joanne. "But when I started reading computer magazines, my husband began to complain about how he had to watch our son while I read.

"My husband says he wants to be supportive of my recovery. Yet sometimes when he clears the table and puts Johnny to bed so I can get to a meeting, he acts like a martyr and tries to make me feel guilty for going.

"I care enough about myself to go to the meeting anyway. But many times I've come home feeling high on the program only to be plummeted to the depths of my disease by an angry, sullen husband."

Part of Joanne's burden stems from the traditional assumption that it's a woman's responsibility to take care of the family's needs. It's often difficult for Joanne, as it is for other women, to ask her husband or her children for help. Women in Joanne's position often have difficulty explaining to their loved ones that they want to go back to school or take a job. They're afraid that if they forge ahead in pursuing personal goals, they will be criticized, rejected, or even abandoned. Guilt takes over.

Joanne (who feels that "guilt" is her middle name) explains: "My 'real job,' for which I'm not paid, is at home. But I am paid and receive more recognition and respect for my other 'real job' at the office. When I wanted to take a home-decorating course, nobody in the family objected. But when I wanted to learn computer programming, to advance my career, you should have seen the fireworks.

"My mother-in-law refused to baby-sit for the kids, saying 'Isn't it enough that you work all day and go to O.A. too? Do you have to go out another night? Who is going to mother those kids and take care of that husband of yours? Put your career off for later and stop going to O.A. so much. You aren't fat anymore anyway!' But when I took the home-decorating course, she thought it was 'great.'

"I'm surprised that her guilt trip sunk in, that it's still hard for me to do things for me, just for me. I was brought up to think that I belonged to the family, not myself. I thought I had outgrown all that. I guess I haven't. But I'm going to go ahead and take the computer course anyway."

Joanne began the course and, much to her delight, found that not only did her family eventually accept her absence, they became proud of her for tackling a difficult task. Even her mother-in-law (although she still grumbled) began to boast about what a smart daughter-in-law she had. In addition, the course filled an intellectual hunger in Joanne, which lessened her need for food.

Sex-role Pressures

Sex-role pressures may lead us to use food to calm tensions. This can be destructive to both overeaters, who put on excessive weight, and bulimics, who purge, abuse laxatives, or use enemas because of the cultural imperative to stay thin at all costs. Compulsive eating robs us of time, energy, money, and good health — resources needed to achieve goals. It also destroys our self-confidence, which is essential to our success. When the disease takes over, our performance suffers, which increases anxiety. This may lead to even more bingeing and purging, as the vicious cycle continues.

In O.A. we hear slogans such as "easy does it," "first things first," and "keep it simple." Complicated food plans and over-extended schedules spell disaster for our abstinence and our peace-of-mind. If we put ourselves under too much stress or live for others, it's only a matter of time until we regress into our illness.

Conflicts between home roles and career goals must be openly acknowledged and discussed with an O.A. sponsor, an O.A. friend, or a professional therapist. They shouldn't be submerged by food and left unresolved.

Peter's Story

Not only women are bothered by these conflicts. Men also have conflicts between their careers and families. Their difficult choices may also not be well-received by others.

Peter, for instance, decided to request two weeks of leave so he could be with his wife following the birth of their second child. He felt he had missed much of the joy of becoming a father the first time because he was too busy overeating — and overworking. As part of his recovery in O.A., he came to deeply value his relationships at home and was no longer willing to sacrifice his family life for money or successes.

Yet, Peter was hesitant. Many times his boss had made it clear that he expected his workers to make their jobs their first priority in life. Prior to O.A., Peter typically pleased the boss by working long hours and weekends. Also, his identity was heavily dependent on the size of his paycheck, rather than on the quality of his human relationships. As his paycheck grew larger and larger, so did Peter. Because he was working so hard, he felt entitled to many extra snacks and huge dinners, which he usually ate alone.

When Peter contracted diabetes and found O.A., he realized that despite all the rich food he had devoured and all the money he had made, he was poor indeed. Not only did he have few friends, but he had allowed himself to become married to the office, rather than to his wife. His daughter, as well as his nephews and nieces, were almost strangers to him. He knew more about his secretary's family than he did his own. Clearly, his compulsive overeating was, in part, a substitute for the family life and friendships that could be enriching if he made changes in his priorities.

As part of his amends to himself and to his family, Peter stopped working overtime, except when absolutely necessary. He also began to attend his daughter's school plays and took her to the doctor's office. He was determined to enjoy the rest of his daughter's childhood as much as possible, and to witness the birth of his second child.

Peter's request for leave, however, was greeted with disbelief and ridicule. "Henpecked, aren't you?" smirked the boss. "What are you going to do, help change diapers?" asked a colleague, laughing.

As a child, Peter had been called "wimp" and "sissie" not only because he was obese, but because he was emotionally sensitive and had intellectual interests. Also, he wasn't athletic and refused to bully others. Since he couldn't prove his manhood physically, he had tried to prove it in school by achieving intellectually and, later in life, by becoming financially successful and working long hours.

In O.A. he was learning to slowly let go of these measures of self-worth and to invest more of himself in his relationships. There would be no salary increase for being a good father, no applause at the staff meeting for being a caring husband or a giving O.A. member. Nevertheless, Peter felt he had to pay attention to his relationships and his feelings, for ignoring them had contributed greatly to his compulsive overeating and his diabetes.

Organizing his life around his emotions was a new and frightening matter for Peter. Like some men, Peter had been taught that only women were guided by their feelings, and therefore, women were "weak." In contrast, men were guided by logic.

Standing in his boss's office, feeling taunted and emasculated, Peter thought he should tell his boss that his request for paternity leave was just a joke and announce that he would work overtime that night. But visions of the mounds of food he used to devour while working overtime flooded Peter's consciousness. Peter remembered that he had to be true to himself, no matter what the cost.

That night Peter had an anxiety attack. Fearing that he would be demoted, or even fired, he had an old-fashioned, pre-O.A. binge.

"Forget the binge," his sponsor said. "Don't project about the future; instead, congratulate yourself for having the courage to stand up for yourself. You're a pioneer, not a sissie."

Peter was not fired or demoted. But he wasn't promoted either. Since the company saw Peter as having divided loyalties, it preferred to promote men who were single-heartedly devoted to the job. "That hurt," says Peter. "Yet in O.A., I'm realizing that I can't have it all. Just like I can't eat everything I want and keep my health, I can't be a superstar at work and also maintain my abstinence and close family ties."

Setting Boundaries

We often have as much trouble saying "no" to others as we do saying "no" to food. When we do say "no," we often feel guilty and then eat to forget the guilt. In O.A., however, we learn to put limits not only on how much we eat, but on how much we can give or do for others.

Setting limits on relationships is not easy for us, since we often fear we'll be rejected or emotionally abandoned if we don't give to others or do as they wish. Some of us feel so unworthy and insecure that we assume we'll not be loved unless we give, give, give, and then give some more.

Some of us grew up in families where we adopted, or were given, the role of family peacemaker or comforter. If we grew up in alcoholic homes, perhaps we were "little adults" as children and took on adult roles with our siblings and alcoholic parents. In such cases, it's hard for us to break away from the caretaker role. In fact, we may come to adopt a "let me take care of you" posture in other relationships. While helping and giving to others are beautiful qualities, problems arise when we give too much to others and, in the process, neglect ourselves. When we overextend ourselves for others, we may end up taking care of ourselves by overeating.

In O.A. we learn that we can't "be there" for others unless we're there for ourselves. Usually this requires that we follow the O.A. recovery program. We also learn that it is as good to give to ourselves as it is to give to others. We are also given the courage to say "no" to unacceptable requests and behavior, such as verbal and physical abuse.

Our recovery is one of our major priorities. One day at a time, we must do whatever is needed to maintain abstinence from compulsive eating. We may need to attend a meeting, make phone calls, write, or meditate even when these actions conflict with another's demands for our time. Many of us have learned the hard way — through relapse — that our ability to give to others is directly proportional to our ability to give to ourselves.

Accepting Anger

Anger is an uncomfortable emotion for most people — especially for us, since we often eat to appease our anger. Despite popular psychology books that often suggest to "let your anger out," sanctions against expressing anger still exist. Many of us were raised to believe that anger is a sin. As children, we may have been punished for displaying anger toward our parents, teachers, siblings, or others.

Abstinence from compulsive eating may bring our negative emotions to the surface, leaving us with the problem of how to direct their powerful energy into constructive channels. To be whole persons, we must own all of ourselves, even our negative side. We can't suppress negative feelings toward others forever. No matter how much food we eat or how much we deny things, negative feelings are bound to emerge. It's better that they be expressed to an O.A. friend, a therapist, or a Higher Power, than be turned inward on the self. One of the major causes of suicidal depressions can be traced to repressed anger. Often when we say, "I'm depressed," we really mean "I'm angry" or "I'm resentful."

Yet anger is a normal human emotion. If we have been violated or abused, emotions such as rage or hate are appropriate. But some of us keep anger to ourselves. Often we fail to catch our anger when it begins. In this case, only when anger has built up to rage do we notice it. Then, fearing that our volcano of rage will erupt, we stifle all our angers, both large and small.

Jane's Story

"I'm so ashamed of being so angry," says Jane, who suffers from years of suppressed anger. Usually Jane, like many of us, doesn't realize she is angry until two or three days after an incident. By that time she has binged. Then, furious with herself for bingeing, she eats even more. The excess food dulls her emotions and her mind, making her less capable of effectively dealing with the problem that sparked her anger.

"There's so much anger in me, I don't know where to start," Jane often says in meetings, pointing to her heavy thighs, which, she feels, are primarily the result of years of suppressed anger.

For Jane, recognizing she is angry (instead of hungry) and allowing herself to be angry are monumental achievements. She now feels she has the right to be angry when insulted, rather than to assume that she is unworthy of some respect and consideration.

Jane has also found it essential to release her anger physically. All emotions have a physical component, but especially anger and rage. When we are angry, our adrenaline and blood pressure levels rise. There is an increase in our energy level that needs to be released through exercise or some other constructive physical activity. Writing about the anger or speaking about the anger also help, especially if we can't or choose not to confront the person who made us mad.

Many of us fear dealing with anger because we're overwhelmed with the prospect of dealing with years of stored up hurts and resentments. But just as we don't have to eliminate all of our character defects at once, neither do we have to deal with all our anger at once. We can deal with anger in small, manageable doses. In meditation, we can seek guidance from our Higher Power as to which angers to deal with first. Acknowledging our anger doesn't necessarily mean we have to act on it. We may choose not to share our angry feelings with a particular person. For example, it may be good not to express our raw anger toward a supervisor (if we need the job) or to a friend or relative who may respond violently.

Yet, persistent or extreme anger toward a particular person is a signal that some of our basic needs aren't being met in that relationship and changes may be needed. Some of us fear that admitting anger in a relationship will lead to its demise. Often, the opposite is true. Usually it's the long-term repression of anger by either person that more often leads to the end of the relationship.

Anger is a frequent topic at O.A. meetings because, for us, anger is a two-faced devil. On the one hand, if we deny our anger we're bound to suffer and eventually eat over it. On the other hand, we can't stay abstinent or live fully in the present if we hold on to our angers and resentments. "Anger is the dubious luxury of normal people," we often hear at meetings. Yet this doesn't mean that we are to be so holy as to never be angry, but rather that we need to take physical, emotional, and spiritual steps toward resolving our anger and ultimately, toward letting go of it.

Emotionally, our work is to acknowledge our anger and feel its heat. Physically, we may need to talk or write about it, or punch a pillow or yell into empty space. Spiritually, we may need to pray for the willingness to let go of the anger and for the health and success of the person who is the target of our rage. This is perhaps the hardest act of all: praying for someone we may still resent, especially if that person has hurt or betrayed us.

Sandra's Story

Sandra had every reason to hate her ex-husband. He had mistreated her and her three children throughout the marriage. After she left him, he gave her little child support and in many other ways made her life as miserable as possible. She came to O.A. many pounds overweight and bulimic, but she claimed that she had already forgiven her husband.

"I'll believe that when you're abstinent," her sponsor said. Her efforts at forgiveness, although sincere, were superficial because she had never acknowledged her anger toward her former spouse. All her life, she felt, she had never been angry at anyone. Anger was "bad" in her view and wasn't a problem for her. Besides, she wasn't in O.A. to deal with anger, only with her ten to eleven P.M., nonstop eating binges.

46

In taking her Step Four inventory, however, Sandra realized she had many angers and hurts. When her repressed anger began to surface, she became, in her own words, "a blaze of hate."

"I was so full of fury I wanted to kill! In the past, I used to get depressed thinking about my ex-husband. Now I was fantasizing planting explosives under his car, putting a knife in his heart, and hurting his new girlfriend too, not caring if I went to jail and left my children motherless."

For almost nine months, all Sandra could talk about at meetings was her anger. But she thought she was making progress because she was finally feeling her anger. But her growth was incomplete — she was having more problems with food. She would be abstinent for two or three days, but then start bingeing again. After four years in the program, her binges weren't as large as in the days prior to O.A., but they were still binges.

Sandra was inadvertently allowing her anger toward her ex-husband to affect her relationships with male friends and male colleagues at work, though they had nothing to do with the abuses she had endured while married. Also, she was freely sharing her rage with her children.

"For people like us, it's either forgive or self-destruct. There's nothing in between," her sponsor said, suggesting that Sandra read "Freedom from Bondage" in the book, *Alcoholics Anonymous*. There, Sandra found the following recommendation:

> If you have a resentment you want to be free of,
> if you will pray for the person or thing that you
> resent, you will be free. If you will ask in prayer for
> everything you want for yourself to be given to
> them, you will be free. Ask for their health, their
> prosperity, their happiness, and you will be free.
> Even when you don't really want it for them, and
> your prayers are only words and you don't mean it,

go ahead and do it anyway. Do it every day for two weeks and you will find you have come to mean it and to want it for them, and you will realize that where you used to feel bitterness and resentment and hatred, you now feel compassionate understanding and love.

Sandra balked. She could not — would not — pray for the man who had been her abuser. Yet it was obvious to many, including Sandra herself, that although her anger was justifiable, it was killing her, not her ex-husband. Out of necessity, Sandra forced herself to get on her knees and pray for her ex-husband.

As Sandra prayed for the willingness to let go of the anger, sadness for the sorrows she had experienced replaced the anger that had once filled her heart. She realized then that her pain went way back, prior to her marriage and to her relationships with her parents and others. To some extent, she had made her ex-husband the scapegoat for all the other people in her life she felt had hurt her. Sandra's anger at her ex-husband had been a defense, not only against her pain, but against recognizing that many resentments and disappointments were buried underneath her food obsession.

By having the courage to suffer honestly, rather than via the food compulsion, Sandra has become freer to embrace her life in the present and has achieved a new level of physical recovery. For example, today she can separate her feelings toward men in the present from her feelings toward her ex-husband. When she becomes annoyed with a man, she can now ask herself, *Am I this upset with this particular man for something he did, or is most of my anger toward him due to my ex-husband?*

After working hard to attain an attitude of forgiveness toward her ex-husband, Sandra thought she was finally finished with him and with all anger and pain. But when her ex-husband began to harass her again, Sandra's anger began to rear its ugly head. Her murderous fantasies returned, as did her nighttime eating.

"I've touched the savage in me again," Sandra told her sponsor. "Now what do I do?"

"Start all over again: Step One, Step Two, Step Three, et cetera," was the reply.

The last piece of anger to be worked on was Sandra's gloating over her ex-husband's misfortunes. *I'm not saying or doing anything against him,* she thought. *So it must be okay to feel this way. After all the times he's made me suffer, I'm entitled to enjoy watching him suffer a little bit too.*

Sandra eventually realized that relishing her ex-husband's mishaps, while perfectly normal, was a way of keeping him in her life. Also, the time and energy she spent thinking about him was draining her emotionally.

As she continued to work the spiritual part of the O.A. program, Sandra detached from her ex-husband to such a degree that she considered him just another person, not someone to get even with.

Sandra has had to deal with her anger many times. Today she feels her anger more quickly than when she first joined O.A. She knows that she doesn't need to work the Steps perfectly to have much of her anger lifted. All that's required is that she make an honest effort and ask for help. She has learned that her forgiveness doesn't have to be perfect, constant, or complete for her to maintain physical abstinence and emotional serenity.

Ending Relationships

Accepting and dealing with anger was difficult for Sandra. But even more difficult for her, and for many of us, is accepting and dealing with losses, especially with losses in relationships. There are no Steps or prayers that can bring back the dead or restore the people we've lost due to time, relocation, personal misunderstanding, rejection, or desertion. What we can do is ask our Higher Power for the willingness and serenity to accept the loss and the strength and support to endure the inevitable grief, one day at a time.

As compulsive eaters, many of us have used our food addiction to cope with the profound sense of sorrow that results from losing people. Parents must face the loss of their children once they mature and move away from home and the loss of their spouse's undivided attention once a child is born.

Losing people might seem to violate our sense of control. We have to face the fact that we are powerless over other people's lives. For example, as much as we might love a particular person, we can't protect that person from illness or death. Neither can we save people from their problems or control their emotions or the events of their lives.

But we sometimes do try to influence others to give up a certain involvement or interest or not to change. Initially our attempts to hold on to that person may be successful, but eventually our efforts backfire. At one point or another that person will come to resent our intrusion and begin to withdraw. If we are too domineering we may lose our relationship with that person entirely. As we often hear in O.A. meetings, the paradox is that the only way to hold on to people is to let them go.

Of course, letting go of people — losing people to their own lives or to their Higher Power's will for them — is much easier said than done. It takes much effort and a willingness to feel the pain of separation. Barbara was jealous of her daughter when her daughter turned thirteen. Barbara began nibbling after dinner, a habit she had given up after joining O.A. Ten pounds and ten O.A. phone calls later, Barbara realized she was eating in response to her daughter's growing up.

"What my daughter is doing is all so normal," Barbara told her sponsor. "Why can't I adjust?"

"Turn the situation around and look at the positive," the sponsor said. "Isn't your daughter's growth beautiful? Didn't you play a part in producing such a mentally and physically healthy child? Would you really want her to have no friends but you, to be dependent on you, glued to you? What if your daughter sat around the kitchen all night eating instead of being with friends? Then you really would have a problem."

Barbara was also encouraged to view her daughter's increased absences as occasions to have time for herself. Later in her journal, Barbara wrote, "Yes, it is natural and good that my daughter grow away from me, and I can learn to see this as a time of freedom for me. But the feelings of loss overwhelm me. I wonder if my ego can take the fact that I must now recede in importance in her life."

Mourning Losses

Our sense of loss is most profound when we must confront the death of a loved one. Divorce or the break up of a long-term love relationship involves the mourning process. Death and divorce are two of the major causes of relapse among O.A. members. At such times we may be coping not only with the pain and anger involved, but also with the financial hardship and social isolation. A widow may find herself without many of the friends she used to have and perhaps with fewer funds than before. Similarly, divorced people suffer from loneliness as well as a tighter budget. We can easily respond to these traumas by compulsive eating.

According to Dr. Elisabeth Kübler-Ross, author of *On Death and Dying,* a landmark book on the psychology of dying, the grieving process consists of five stages: denial or shock, anger, bargaining, depression, and acceptance. These stages don't always occur in order and a person can be in more than one stage at the same time. In the first stage, denial or shock, we don't acknowledge the loss. If we're compulsively eating, it's all that much easier to pretend that the loved one isn't dead or gone. But once we face the reality of the loss, we may become enraged. "Why me?" we may shout to life, or to our Higher Power. "Isn't it enough that I have a problem with food; do I have to lose my loved one too?"

We may also be angry at the departed. "Why did you have to go die and leave me alone?" we may shout. We may also be angry at ourselves for thinking how we may have hurt or offended our loved one.

During the bargaining stage, we bargain with our Higher Power and ourselves. This stage is filled with the *if only's.* "If only I had done that, they wouldn't have died or left."

We can't resurrect the dead, nor can we force someone to love us. Realizing the impotency of both our anger and our bargaining, we may become depressed and bitter. Following the stage of depression comes acceptance. Acceptance is more than resignation; however, like resignation, it involves much sadness.

Sharon's Story

For a long time Sharon put off mourning her father's death. Her husband had left her at about the same time, and with the adjustments of becoming a single parent she didn't feel she had time to think about her father's death.

"Yet when I was alone with myself, I'd feel so anxious and empty that I'd run from one place to the next, stopping at fast food places all along the way," Sharon says. "Finally I had to sit down and face it. 'I miss you Papa. Where are you now? I still need you. Come back to me. I'm sorry I hurt you those times,' I'd cry to the wall.

"Every pore in my body hurt and I couldn't make the hurt go away. 'This too shall pass,' O.A. people told me. *But when?* I wondered. I didn't know I had that much pain in me."

In relapse, Sharon learned that she wasn't in control of her pain. Even though she did a lot of recovery work — talking to her sponsor, attending O.A. meetings, praying, writing — she couldn't make the pain go away. *It takes as long as it takes,* she concluded. That night she had a dream in which the stages of grief were depicted:

"I was on a beach looking for my father. Even though I knew he was dead, I kept thinking I would find him because he loved the water. I was so happy on that beach, pretending he was alive [Denial]. I even put some gifts for him on the shore, hoping the gifts would bring him back [Bargaining]. Suddenly huge tidal waves came and washed away my gifts. I shouted at the waves and tried to fight them [Anger], but they were too powerful for me. I got lost in the pain. When I woke up, I realized my father was truly gone and nothing I could do would bring him back [Acceptance]."

If we have truly loved someone, we may always miss them. But reaching the stage of acceptance signifies that much of our grief work has been completed and that we can move on to other things in life.

Yet those of us who have lost a beloved parent, spouse, or child may think of that person every day. Anniversaries or special days associated with that person may bring about increased sadness and increased eating.

At such moments we must remember that we are powerless over food and that it's okay to feel sad. We may think that food has power — power to solve our problems, power to take away our hurts, power to make our life the way we want it. We may also think that being thin has power — power to make our life pain-free. But no matter what we eat or don't eat, no matter if we gorge, stay abstinent, or starve ourselves, we can't bring back the past, the person, or relationship we treasured and have lost.

Grieving our losses requires much courage and suffering. The only way to ultimately lessen the pain and to keep it from paralyzing us is to work through it. Like it or not, if we ever want to be emotionally alive to the present, we must be willing to walk through the valley of our sadness and tears.

PART 3

Special Kinds Of Relationships

Critical Persons

Critical persons and negative criticism may strike terror in our hearts. We may also listen to the well-established critic who lives inside our own head. Often this internal critic torments us by repeating, *You should be perfect. You should be perfect.* And when we fall short of perfection, it says, *See, I told you you were no good and can't do anything right.*

But this critical voice is mistaken. One critical remark about our behavior or work isn't a final judgement that we're inept, incompetent, or unlovable people. A sign of our recovery is the ability to accept negative feedback without blowing it out of proportion. Hopefully we will learn to appreciate valid criticism and be willing to grow from it.

Just as we learn to accept legitimate criticism from others, we also come to view our food slips, or even our relapses, not as the end of the world, but as part of a learning process. We can learn something about ourselves — our innermost needs and deepest fears — from our slips. Meanwhile, our O.A. friends continually remind us that despite having binged or relapsed, we're still lovable, worthwhile, recovering people.

Responding to Negative Comments

Friends, family members, and others who don't understand or who refuse to understand the nature and seriousness of our illness often leave us frustrated, angry, and feeling ashamed. We need to learn how to detach from negative or ignorant comments. We may also decide to directly deal with those who openly mock us, if we feel doing so is in our best interest.

For example, when Laura visited her family during school break, they all congratulated her on her obvious weight loss. She was no Slenderella, but that F.A. or A.O. or whatever it was had certainly done wonders. But when Laura began to weigh and measure her food, she heard comments like, "You really are a food addict, aren't you?" or, "Why do you still need to do that?" said another. "You look okay now — almost — except for those hips. They'll probably always be big." Another relative pointed to Laura's slightly protruding stomach.

Why are you all looking at my body, not at me? Laura wanted to yell. *And what would you rather me be doing than measuring my food: bingeing my brains out around here, like I used to?* Instead, she went into the bathroom and cried. *Why did I come here?* she wondered.

In the bathroom (one of her old eating spots), Laura resolved not to eat over her family's reactions. She kept repeating to herself, *I am a good person even if my hips will never be small. I am a good person, even if they make fun of me and don't understand. I am a good person, even if I do have an eating disorder.*

At that moment, Laura hated her family. Yet it was the only family she had and she truly did love them. Was there any way she could make them understand?

At first Laura considered giving her family an elaborate description of the disease of compulsive eating and a detailed analysis of her problems with food addiction. But Laura decided that a long lecture wouldn't be needed, especially since telling her food secrets might make her family feel guilty and make her vulnerable to further cutting remarks.

Perhaps in the future I can share with my family more openly, Laura decided. For now, she believed it best to matter-of-factly state that she had a problem with food and that weighing and measuring her meals, even while on a family vacation, was something she needed to do. If her family wanted to know more about O.A. and eating disorders, she would gladly discuss the matter with them.

Joyce's Story

Sometimes we are singled out for attention and ridicule, not by family members, but by colleagues or bosses at work. During her first year in O.A., Joyce lost almost 70 pounds. But after three years of abstinence, she began to relapse due to family problems. Yet Joyce had a strong emotional and spiritual program and was confident that as long as she kept coming back to meetings and tried to work the Steps, she would soon regain her physical abstinence and lose the desired weight.

At work, however, Joyce's hard-earned self-confidence was being shaken by a slender co-worker who gloated at Joyce's weight gain. Not only did this co-worker make comments about Joyce's increasing size (in front of other staff and the clients) but at times she would put forbidden snacks in front of Joyce and ask Joyce if she would like to have some. In addition, this woman made a point of talking about diets whenever Joyce walked into the room.

Joyce tried to focus on her work and ignore the co-worker, but the co-worker kept intruding on Joyce's space with her comments and her cookies. Joyce tried to be polite and, in prayer, turn the situation over to her Higher Power. "I've got to let it go," she kept saying at meetings. Yet many nights she came home wanting to "kill" her co-worker. Instead, she "killed" herself with large predinner snacks.

"Can you muster whatever self-love you have left and stand up for yourself?" an O.A. friend inquired.

Like many of us, Joyce didn't like confrontations. Angry voices and angry faces frightened her. Joyce felt paralyzed in taking action because the co-worker had brought up many of her old feelings of self-hate for being a compulsive eater, feelings which O.A. had helped bury long ago. *I'm a compulsive eater and in relapse; therefore, I deserve abuse,* she thought.

Joyce was prepared to suffer in silence until the co-worker began to laugh whenever Joyce sat in a chair. "I wonder if the chair is going to break today," she'd say.

At this point, with the support of her O.A. friends, Joyce decided she had to be assertive. She would ask the co-worker to refrain from making any more comments about her weight and appearance. If the co-worker persisted in tormenting her, she would simply pull out a pad of paper, document the abuse, and then, in her most calm voice, say, "Excuse me, but I'm just checking my notes here. Am I correct in noting that you just called me (such and such) or did (such and such)?"

If this approach didn't stop the co-worker, Joyce resolved to discuss the matter with her supervisor. Although she didn't want this co-worker to control her life, if necessary, she would look for a new job.

Our critics may not be as insensitive as Laura's family or as vicious as Joyce's co-worker. But under no circumstances should we internalize their humiliating remarks about our weight or appearance. Neither should we allow the ridicule of uninformed and cruel people to deter us from pursuing our goals. Perhaps we can get courage from Bob, whose management trainer made frequent degrading comments about his weight, even in front of his colleagues. Bob was able to overlook most of such remarks, until the day the trainer accused him of having emotional problems. "If you weren't such a psychological mess, you wouldn't be so fat," he said.

Bob fled from the classroom in tears, vowing to quit his job and abandon his dream of becoming a manager rather than endure more humiliation. He was ashamed at having openly wept, but he was more ashamed about being overweight. He was so ashamed he didn't even want to share his experience at his O.A. home meeting. But his caring O.A. friend sensed his pain, and encouraged him to talk.

"Don't let him destroy you!" they shouted. "He's not worth it." Many at the meeting were in tears, for they had been similarly degraded. One O.A. member, a bulimic, had just been at a family dinner party where jokes were made about whether or not she vomited with a straw, a spoon, or just her bony red finger.

If we have been victimized by verbal or other forms of abuse due to our weight or food habits, we need not be so ashamed of ourselves that we fail to reach out to our O.A. and other understanding friends for support. Many in O.A. have suffered from similar forms of discrimination.

Problems in O.A. Relationships: Dependency

O.A. is a program of many seeming contradictions. For example, we're told that only by admitting our powerlessness over food can we obtain some degree of control over our eating. We're also told that the only way to "hold on" to people is to "let go" of them.

Many of us hear in meeting after meeting that O.A. is a "we," not an "I," program and that it's a sign of recovery to turn to people, rather than to food, in time of need. Yet, in the back of our minds, we might secretly resist the notion that we are truly powerless over food or that we really need the people in O.A. All we need, we may think, is a few weight control tips and a little moral support to get us over the hump. After a few meetings, we will certainly be back on our own two feet again.

Although we come to O.A. looking for help, we may find it difficult to ask for help by getting a sponsor or making phone calls. Or, if we do have a sponsor, perhaps we don't call often and share only part of ourselves, never fully revealing our food or other "secrets."

Some of us faithfully follow the recommendation of making O.A. calls when emotionally upset, troubled by food thoughts or cravings, or when tempted to binge. Yet we may always try to call different people so that no one person would ever get to know us. Or perhaps we make O.A. calls only when we feel strong, never when we feel desperate.

In admitting our powerlessness over food and our need for others, we may fear we'll be branded as weak, childlike, or emotionally immature. Yet a major root of the food addiction is the irrational belief that to be a true adult we must rely only on our strength, intellect, and powers — at all times. Another belief is that feeling helpless, confused, afraid, or in need of assistance are signs of failure. How many of us have compulsively eaten to shove our dependency needs out of awareness or to punish ourselves for having such needs? Some of us are shocked to find that after reaching out for help, we reach for food. Inside we're telling ourselves, *What's the matter with me? I should be able to do it on my own.* Yet we might gladly spend hours on the phone with an O.A. member who needs help, never once condemning our friend for feeling fragile or afraid.

In O.A. we humbly learn that we need others, not only to help us fight our disease, but to help us deal with life itself. It's far healthier for us to admit to our dependency needs (even if they are extreme) rather than to hide behind a facade of independence.

"My main problem in life," says Jim, "was that I hated to admit that I needed anybody. It was all fine and good to hear in meetings that what bound us together was not our strengths but our weaknesses. But to actually admit that I couldn't handle my food, my feelings, or my relationships, was unthinkable.

"For two years I sat in meetings feeling superior to all the others in O.A. who seemed so needy. When they talked about having to call their sponsor twice a day or make five phone calls in one night, I thought, *Hah! I'll never have to do that.*

"But they were losing weight and I wasn't. And after a twenty pound weight gain — in, not out of, the program — I finally broke down and got a food sponsor.

"Now I'm as greedy for help as I used to be for food. In fact, I now have three sponsors: a food sponsor, a Step sponsor, and a relationships sponsor. I go to open Al-Anon meetings too, to get help with my relationships, even though no one in my family is an alcoholic.

"To think that I was once too proud to call or to go to two meetings a day. These days I can't wait to get to the phone or a meeting. It's such a relief not to feel I have to figure out everything, from what to eat, to how to handle my boss, all by myself."

Sponsors

Problems can arise when we become overly dependent on specific people in O.A. rather than on the O.A. program as a whole or on our Higher Power. If we have made sponsors our Higher Power, we may expect them to have all the answers. When sponsors can't solve our problems for us, or when they make mistakes, we may become resentful. We may decide never to share with them again, or even to quit O.A. But it's important to discuss grievances with a sponsor as we would with any other person.

We may also want to examine unrealistic expectations we might have of our sponsor. We may unconsciously be expecting our sponsor to be the wonderful parent, friend, or spouse we never had or to otherwise provide us with an ideal relationship. Or perhaps we want our sponsor to always be available to us, to always give us unconditional love and acceptance, and to give us unlimited amounts of time and attention.

But our sponsors have needs and pressures of their own. They don't have a magic wand that will make us abstinent and work the Steps for us. They are neither all-knowing nor all-powerful. We shouldn't ask our sponsors to make our decisions for us. Any advice they give should be made in terms of program principles, applying one of the Twelve Steps to a particular problem or relationship.

A related problem is that of O.A. sponsors who attempt to control us or who criticize us in such a manner so as to inhibit our growth. Some sponsors have difficulty tolerating strong emotions. When we are depressed, sad, or angry, they may make unhelpful responses such as, "You shouldn't feel that way," or "Why can't you get over this?" or in other ways blame us for our problems.

Some sponsors become frustrated when we have a relapse or don't make fast enough progress. While sponsors may choose to be as helpful as possible, they can't assume responsibility for anyone's recovery. In addition, if we somehow negatively affect our sponsor's growth or are unwilling to make efforts to work the program, a sponsor should be able to discontinue his or her role without guilt.

Jo was glad to sponsor Pam until Pam stopped going to meetings and reading O.A. literature. Pam also insisted on describing her food binges in great detail, despite Jo's request that she not mention specific foods. When Jo suggested that Pam try to get help from more than one person in O.A., Pam refused and insisted on calling Jo twice a day instead.

Jo continued to sponsor Pam for a long time, primarily out of guilt. But when Pam started yelling at her for not making her better faster, Jo finally ended the relationship. Jo also had to end a sponsoring relationship with an O.A. member who was suicidal and refused to seek professional help. Jo believed she couldn't take responsibility for another O.A. member's life. Neither could she always be on call during an O.A. member's frequent suicidal crises. When an O.A. member is severely depressed or suicidal or is suffering from one or more problems other than food addiction, it's wise for a sponsor to recommend professional help.

"When I first started sponsoring, I wanted to fix everybody in sight," says Jo. "But now I realize that my main job is to listen and to communicate that I care. In listening, I allow people to hear themselves. I may have a perspective to offer or a program suggestion, but I don't have all the answers. All I can do is point people to their Higher Power, if they have one, and to the Steps."

Limit Setting

Whether or not we are sponsors, we may overextend ourselves in our work, family, and O.A. relationships. If we neglect ourselves or other important priorities to help an O.A. friend or provide service to the program, we may end up bingeing, depressed, or both.

Georgia had to set limits on how many people she could sponsor and on the length and number of phone calls she could receive per day. She had particular problems with an O.A. friend who would always call her late at night, just before bedtime. "This person was a newcomer and in so much pain, I just couldn't say no to him," Georgia explains. But Georgia was also tired of being "the big ear" and her sleep was suffering. On a couple of occasions, Georgia even found herself eating after the phone call.

Eventually, Georgia had to ask newcomers to call earlier and limit their phone calls to a half hour. Thus, she kept her commitment to O.A. service without affecting her recovery.

Critical O.A. Members

We may be more easily hurt by critical remarks made by O.A. members than those made by people outside of O.A. In O.A. we expect to be accepted, understood, and loved by others who are like us.

We learn in O.A. to accept the faults and mistakes of our family members, friends, and others outside O.A. Yet when someone in O.A. makes a belittling remark about our appearance, about our progress in the program, or about something we shared at a meeting, we might be tempted to either break down, retaliate, or never come back to O.A.

For example, when Jane shared her feelings about her brother at an O.A. meeting, another O.A. member whispered in her ear, "Sounds like an unresolved sibling rivalry complex to me. Have you considered intensive psychotherapy?" When Jane shared about her heavy workload and her need to exercise twice a day, this same O.A. member told her, "Sounds compulsive to me."

Jane was angry but said nothing, primarily because the O.A. member who made these remarks had many years of abstinence. In contrast, Jane was still struggling with food.

Like Jane, we may be intimidated by long-term members. Alas, some members may have forgotten from where they came. Or we may have made cutting remarks to newer O.A. members. Such arrogance does not belong in O.A. Many O.A. members who are still overweight may have gained a satisfying degree of emotional and spiritual recovery. To judge O.A. members solely by their ability to stay on a particular food plan or by their weight loss contradicts the heart of the O.A. program. We aren't in O.A. to compare ourselves to others, or to judge them. We're in O.A. to learn about and to improve ourselves.

Accepting Our Bodies, Accepting Ourselves

It's common and natural for us to resent and be jealous of people who can eat as much as they want without gaining weight. "I knew I had reached some level of recovery when I looked at a size three blonde with skinny legs and saw her as a child of God rather than somebody who should be dead," states a ten-year member of O.A. Just the week before, this O.A. member had decided to stop worrying about her weight and to love herself despite her lumpy thighs and flabby arms.

Overcoming jealousy and resentment requires that we accept the reality of our illness and our bodies. As painful as it might be, we must accept our bodies the way they are before we can realize self-love and self-acceptance.

Acceptance of our bodies also helps our relationships with those in O.A. who are losing weight faster than we are or who enter the program thin or only slightly overweight. Allison came to O.A. almost 100 pounds overweight and needed nearly seven years to reach goal weight. Only then did she dare to talk to or call O.A. members who had years of abstinence, or to sponsor O.A. members who were smaller than herself. Yet when she began to sponsor Christy, who came into O.A. only twenty pounds overweight, Allison was shocked at the amount of envy and hatred she harbored in her heart.

"I found myself wondering why anyone as thin as Christy needed O.A., and resenting her because she had never been fat like I was. Yet I knew that all this comparing and judging going on in my mind was my disease talking, not me.

"Today, I feel that my Higher Power put Christy in my life to teach me, once again, to accept the compulsive eater in me, the fat me. Until I could love and accept that part of myself — the out-of-control girl who used to binge and kept me fat — I couldn't love or accept the other parts of me, or anyone else.

"Accepting myself the way I am has helped me to see Christy and all the normal or almost normal looking women in O.A. as fellow sufferers rather than as competitors or people who are superior to me."

Acceptance of her disease and her body has also helped Allison deal with people who comment on how fat she used to be or who are jealous of her weight loss.

Work Relationships

We may have had difficulties at work due to reduced efficiency or absences caused by bingeing. In addition, if we isolated ourselves, we may have been seen as loners.

Once in recovery, we might feel uncomfortable joining our co-workers for lunch or other food-oriented events. The sight of an abundance of food (or perhaps our old binge foods) may create uncomfortable cravings. Our co-workers and bosses may not understand our problem and may interpret our absence or discomfort as a rejection of them.

Our sensitivity about our physical appearance may carry over into our work relationships, even when our size or physical attractiveness is irrelevant to the task at hand. Also, if we still have unresolved feelings toward authority figures in the past, our present relationship with bosses may be affected. If we've experienced unfairness and rejection in the past from authority figures, perhaps we fear the same painful experience will repeat itself. In anticipation of the pain, we may become defensive, hostile, or closed. Such a reaction may give our boss a negative attitude toward us.

We may only hear our boss's complaints about our work, and ignore the praise. If we're still overweight, perhaps we attribute our supervisor's complaints about us to our weight. But if we've lost the excess weight, we no longer have that excuse. We must accept our supervisor's remarks at face value. If the remarks are negative, this can be painful, for the criticism can't be traced to our body size but to our personality, skills, or other behaviors we must be responsible for.

Bingeing on Work and Food

Some of us are hardworking and competent, but our efforts don't seem to be recognized. Since we're compulsive eaters we may feel we don't deserve to ask for a raise, a promotion, or some special mention. Because we fail to ask, we often fail to receive the appreciation, status, and material rewards we deserve. Perhaps if we received more rewards on and from our job, we would need to reward ourselves less with food.

A compulsive overeater explains: "For four years I binged almost every night and day. Yet I always showed up for work and did everything they told me to do. I never asked questions or said, 'No, this is too much for me right now.' I kept on accepting one assignment after the next, and ate because I couldn't keep up with all that was expected of me.

"One day I found myself doing the work of almost three people. I probably would have kept on compulsively working until the boss stopped me. 'Why didn't you tell me you were overloaded?' he asked.

"What I didn't tell him, but thought to myself was, because I was bingeing I didn't feel I had the right to speak up about anything."

Special problems arise for those of us who are in food-related jobs. Perhaps we can ask ourselves why we have chosen to work in a bakery or restaurant or to become a gourmet chef. Extra efforts and special precautions may be needed to resist the temptations and cravings aroused by being surrounded by so much food for so many hours.

Special problems also arise for those of us in service occupations: day-care, nursing, mental health, or other, similar help-giving fields. When all day we give, give, give, we might be setting ourselves up to come home and eat, eat, eat. Although, as care-givers, we may have very few chances to take breaks or otherwise take care of ourselves, we must take advantage of every opportunity to do so.

Sexual Relationships

Sexual relationships often pose a threat to compulsive overeaters. If we're still overweight, we may be ashamed of our bodies. If we've lost our excess pounds, we may still have a poor body image or be especially sensitive about our body.

"My sexuality," says Peggy, "is loving myself unconditionally — all of myself." She has lost an enormous amount of weight in O.A. but still has many pounds to go before reaching her desired size. "But I won't lose the rest of my weight until I love myself, and that means not just my soul, but my body," she says.

"Before O.A., I pretended I didn't have a body; I was just a head with this mass below that really didn't belong to me. Yet I said 'yes' to every man who wanted me.

"In O.A., however, I've learned that I have a body and that I have to deal with my body. I've also learned to love this body of mine, even if nobody else does. What's more, today I have a choice. Just like I can say 'no' to food I don't want, I can say 'no' to sexual relationships I don't want. Today, my self-respect and self-esteem matter more to me than being seen as desirable. I also know that I have a lot more to offer a man than my body and that I want a lot more out of sex than a momentary thrill."

As Peggy's recovery illustrates, sexually intimate relationships can bring out not only all our feelings about our bodies and our attractiveness, but many of our emotional needs. When only our physical, but not our emotional, needs are being met in the relationship, we may feel frustrated and disappointed despite the sensual pleasures.

Sometimes, we may use sex as a drug or as an escape from ourselves in the same way we used food. Other times, sexual relationships, while much desired, may force us to confront the misgivings we might have about the morality of certain relationships or sexual practices.

Celeste's Story

Special problems arise when we're sexually rejected because of our body size. If we've been called "elephants," "walruses," "fat slobs" or other names by our sexual partners we may lose interest in sex. If we've been ridiculed about our weight in the past, we may shun sexual relationships in the present, even when, despite our weight, we're pursued by the opposite sex. Unconsciously, we feel we can't possibly be attractive sexually until we reach a certain weight or obtain a certain body image.

All of us can learn something by Celeste's story. She met Tom on a blind date. Since he seemed interested in her, she took the initiative in asking to see him again. "You're too big," he said.

Celeste was stunned. It had taken her eight years in O.A. to lose 80 pounds. Although she was not super-slim, she was not obese either. To still be judged as "fat," after all her progress, hurt deeply.

Her first impulse was to go on a crash diet. But O.A. had taught her that diets don't work. Perhaps she would be slimmer in the future, perhaps not. But in the meantime she wouldn't punish herself either with dieting or with bingeing. She would stay on her regular food plan and say the Serenity Prayer, accepting what she could not change: that there would be men who would reject her for not being a Slenderella.

"The miracle is, I love myself anyway," Celeste says.

PART 4

Using The O.A. Program To Improve Relationships

Spirituality

The O.A. philosophy is that compulsive eating is a three-fold illness: physical, emotional, and spiritual. Physically, we eat too much or in a destructive manner. Emotionally, we use food to suppress our feelings. Spiritually, our compulsive eating shows a lack of faith in the goodness of life and a negative attitude toward ourselves and others.

Honesty is the cornerstone of our recovery. Being honest with ourselves, another person, and our Higher Power about our eating habits is a fundamental spiritual step. Perhaps we can't always be abstinent. But difficult as it might be, we can try to be honest about what we eat, how we eat, or why we feel we're overeating.

We may be dishonest about things other than food. Although we may not eat over our dishonesty immediately, we will probably eventually punish ourselves with food or with other forms of self-abuse for our moral slips. An alternative to self- punishment via food abuse is to deal with our character defects directly by working the Steps, specifically Steps Four through Ten.

In *Alcoholics Anonymous*, it's written, "The spiritual life is not a theory. We have to live it." Yet progress, not perfection, is our motto. "We are not saints. The point is that we are willing to grow along spiritual lines."

O.A. stresses the importance of developing a relationship with a Higher Power, which is essential to recovery. It helps us achieve and maintain abstinence, and helps us gain something even more valuable than a normal-sized body: serenity and a fuller life. In the Seventh Step, for example, we ask our Higher Power to remove our character defects, including our compulsive eating. We make this request not only to be thin and beautiful and look good in new clothes, but to be of greater service to ourselves and others.

"I came for the vanity and stayed for the sanity," many of us say. As we grow spiritually in the program, we realize that weight loss and abstinence from compulsive eating is just the beginning. Our ultimate goals in O.A. are not only to curb our food compulsion, but also to develop our moral character, to find a Higher Power, and to live to good purpose, one day at a time.

"Pick any Higher Power you want," Julie tells newcomers, "as long as your Higher Power is loving, kind, and forgiving and has your best interests at heart." Some of us adopt the concept of God, but not necessarily the God of our childhood faith. Some of us do use the God of our childhood, but modify our childhood concept of God to include more peace and less punishment. Still others of us are agnostics or atheists and see the O.A. group, the O.A. principles, nature, or some other force as our Higher Power. "For me, God stands for Good Orderly Direction," says one O.A. member.

Regardless of how we might define our Higher Power, it's important to have one, for without one, food becomes our Higher Power. Food controls not only our behavior, but also our thoughts and feelings. It may even kill us. As compulsive eaters we need spiritual as well as human help. The crux of the O.A. program is for us to humbly admit that we can't do it alone, that we need a Power greater than ourselves.

For many of us, however, this ego-deflating truth is hard to accept. Despite our repeated harmful experiences with food, we often persist in the notion that we can overcome our addiction by relying on our own resources. While we may be able to control our eating behavior temporarily by "white knuckling it" (relying on ourselves), our success will be short-lived at best. Ultimately, the obsession will overpower us.

Julia's Story

Faith in and reliance on a Higher Power can help us deal with our food addiction. Spirituality begins with humbly admitting our powerlessness over food. Julia resisted the idea of a food plan for years. Now she daily admits to herself, her Higher Power, and usually an O.A. friend that she is a compulsive eater. If she doesn't have a food plan for that day, she prays for the willingness to make one. If she binges, it's part of her spiritual program to swallow her pride and ask her Higher Power for the willingness to forgive herself for the binge and to take the steps necessary to prevent another one. Sometimes Julia prays before each meal: "God, help me to eat appropriately for my recovery today, and to act appropriately in my relationships and in all matters affecting my life."

"O.A. is a one-day-at-a-time program," Julia says. "Just because I was abstinent yesterday or the day before is no guarantee that I'll be abstinent today. I'm always just one bite away from insanity.

"So every morning, I ask my Higher Power for help, not just with my food but with my character defects, my relationships, and my various other problems. I also ask for knowledge of my Higher Power's will for me, for that day and for that day only, and for the power and willingness to carry it out. If all I pray for is physical abstinence, then I am using O.A. like a diet club and my Higher Power like a diet manager.

"Sometimes I only pray for five minutes, but it's the most important five minutes of my day."

Julia also takes several other short Higher Power breaks throughout the day, before tackling a difficult project or meeting with a difficult person. She tries to do O.A. reading and write in her journal each day.

When Julia hears O.A. members talk about rising one or two hours early every morning to read, write, meditate, or pray, she berates herself for not being willing to be more spiritual and chastises herself for not meditating longer. Yet the essence of spirituality isn't any specific action, but rather a reaching out to a Higher Power for guidance and strength. The specific practice that helps us get in touch with our Higher Power, and subsequently with ourselves, is irrelevant. Some of us communicate best with our Higher Power when we are doing some activity like jogging, swimming, writing, cleaning house, or listening to music. Others of us, however, feel we need to be resting in bed, surrounded by quiet, or in a church or synagogue, in order to connect.

For many of us, communication with our Higher Power occurs mainly during O.A. meetings or O.A. phone calls, where we hear our feelings and conflicts being articulated and discussed. We often get a fresh and meaningful perspective on one or more of our concerns.

Part of the spirituality of the O.A. program, as with all Twelve Step programs, is trusting that if we make the effort to increase our conscious contact with our Higher Power, we will be less anxious and our lives will be more serene. Eventually, the answers to our problems will come. Step Eleven recommends prayer and meditation. Some days, however, we may not be willing to pray or meditate. Yet we may be willing to go to a meeting or to make a call.

Because our Higher Power is loving and caring, we can trust that if we're willing to take the first step and go to a meeting, we'll hear at least one thing that we need to hear. We can also trust that if we pick up the phone, on the other end of the line will be someone who cares. That person may not have a solution for our dilemma, but they can encourage us not to eat over it.

If the first several persons we call aren't at home or are too busy to listen, we can humbly keep on phoning until we find a sympathetic ear. Since we must either "share it, or wear it," it's not unheard of to try 15 to 20 persons before giving up. If no one is available, we can pray to our Higher Power. Sometimes the answer arises from within us or comes in the form of an unexpected phone call. Sometimes, however, we'll need to wait patiently.

Expanding Our Spiritual Program

On a day-to-day basis, we need to do what we can to improve our conscious contact with our Higher Power. What we need to do may change over time. During times of inner turmoil or external crisis we may want to expand our spiritual program. At such times, we may need to increase the amount of time we pray, meditate, or attend religious services in order to meet our spiritual needs.

Spirituality, however, isn't a matter of ritual or a matter of following a mechanical or rigid list of "shoulds." We don't need to meditate for so many minutes or write so many pages in a journal. Rather, spirituality is an attitude — an attitude toward life, oneself, and others. It includes humility, honesty, gratitude, self-love, forgiveness, patience, and living in the present.

Spirituality also involves continually taking Steps Three and Eleven and praying for the willingness to follow our Higher Power's will for us, rather than our own. The O.A. message is that there's a purpose for our existence which, at times, transcends human understanding. For some of us, the purpose is readily apparent. For others of us, however, the meaning of our existence and of certain events may become clear only at some future time.

When we're in situations that baffle or hurt us, the program teaches that we're entitled to our feelings: anger, confusion, and pain. We may ask, "Why me, Higher Power? What did I do to deserve this?" The program encourages us to trust that our Higher Power will help us through hard times and help us bear losses and pain.

Our spirituality is also closely linked with the idea of acceptance — acceptance of the people, places, and things we can't change, and acceptance of life's many imperfections. Even if we follow the Steps and have years of perfect abstinence, our lives will not be perfect. Regardless of how spiritual or thin we are, we'll inevitably have our share of sorrows, injustices, and broken dreams, just as we'll have our share of joys and happiness.

Abandoning perfectionistic standards for ourselves, for others, and for life itself is a part of our spiritual growth. This doesn't mean we shouldn't try to improve ourselves or to make life as rich and meaningful as possible. But we must also learn to accept life on life's terms and to accept our weaknesses and the limitations our disease imposes on us.

Sometimes our perfectionism can serve us well by prodding us to work harder to achieve our goals. But usually it makes us spend too much energy trying to make perfect choices, trying to have perfect relationships, and forming unrealistically high standards. Unfortunately, we tend to be perfectionistic about everything. We not only want to be perfect husbands, wives, brothers or sisters, but perfect employees, and perfect O.A. members too.

When we don't meet our godlike standards, we may forget to focus on our good qualities and punish ourselves with excess food. Physically stymied by food, emotionally stymied by self-hate, and spiritually stymied by negativity, we're unable to determine our Higher Power's will for us each day. This can lead to even more frustration and lack of satisfaction, laying the groundwork for even more eating and self-hate.

Spiritual growth requires that we move beyond the black and white world of perfectionism. It also involves learning to accept and celebrate partial successes, partial joys. If we always require the "ultimate" in our relationships, or in our achievements, we're doomed to living a life of disappointments and being closed to others and to our Higher Power.

An important part of our spirituality is being able to live in the here and now. Julia, for instance, measures her recovery not so much by her degree of abstinence, but by her ability to "stay in today" and to "keep on keeping on" despite her numerous fears. Although abstinent, she many times hasn't enjoyed her freedom from the food compulsion because of her fears. Most times, her exaggerating about how future events could go wrong would lead her back into sugar, no matter how many meetings she attended.

But through her spiritual growth, Julia is learning to overcome her fears, not with sugar, but with faith. She now turns her fears over to her Higher Power each day, realizing that most times there is little she can do to prevent fear from materializing. In her view, faith isn't the absence of fear, but facing fear directly. She now trusts that even if the worst happens, she will be given the grace, the strength, and the support she needs to carry on.

Finding a Higher Power

Some of us come to O.A. already having a strong faith or a well-defined Higher Power. Others of us, however, enter the program perplexed by or disenchanted with the idea of God or a Higher Power. Perhaps we equate spirituality with religion. Or we may confuse the idea of a Higher Power with authority figures from our past who may have been unforgiving or cruel to us.

In O.A. we're encouraged to adopt a Higher Power who is for us, not against us; who wants for us only to be ourselves; and who is, at the very least, able to help us stop our food compulsion. Larry, for example, is an agnostic. Yet he believes in some sort of vague Power greater than himself, but only to help him with his food compulsions. "Past that, I don't know," he says. Due to the program, however, Larry is trying to keep an open mind and stay open to spiritual as well as other changes. Over time he, like other O.A. members, may expand his concept of a Higher Power and ask for help in areas of his life other than food.

Arlene, on the other hand, believes in a Higher Power, but "fusses" and rebels against her Higher Power. "I keep wanting to do it my way — even though I know that my way doesn't work." She sees signs that her Higher Power is trying to help her, but she is not quite ready to surrender.

Spiritual help is always available. Our Higher Power is only a prayer or a phone call away. But anger blocks many of us from our Higher Power. Perhaps we blame our Higher Power for certain misfortunes, or for our food compulsion. More than one of us has asked, "Higher Power, if you truly love me, why did you make me a compulsive eater?" or "Why don't you help me lose weight faster?"

We do not need to hold in our anger. We can talk to our Higher Power about it. In fact, we can share all our thoughts and feelings with our Higher Power, without fear of retaliation or abandonment. After all, we wouldn't be human if we weren't discontent with our Higher Power sometimes.

While our Higher Power is constant in caring for us, our relationship with our Higher Power may have some ups and downs. Even if our faith is strong, we'll undoubtedly experience periods of spiritual doubt and emptiness. We may feel as if our Higher Power isn't listening or that the answers are either unacceptable or too slow in coming.

At such times, we need to persist in going through the motions of keeping conscious contact, even if we don't feel it's worth the effort. If we do the work to connect with our Higher Power, we can build good lines of communication.

In our dealings with other people, a strong spiritual program is essential. Each day, many of us turn our friends, family members, and other loved ones over to the care of our Higher Power. We can't change them. Our Higher Power can. In this way we reduce our anxiety about our relationships and free ourselves of the burden of making all the decisions.

Our tendency has often been to try to control relationships. But only by letting go of the inclination to control others will we know peace. This doesn't mean we should be passive in our relationships and not make necessary decisions. Giving up control means saying that we can't force another person to conform to our will, or to our pressing need.

If we didn't have a Higher Power or a spiritual program to lean on, we might become desperate when our relationships take a turn for the worse. Our spiritual program can help us work on these relationships one at a time, rather than trying to work on them all at once and becoming overwhelmed.

Sandra's Story

Sandra used prayer to help her separate her reactions to the men in her life from her bad feelings toward her father and ex-husband. In addition, she found that by surrendering her economic and job problems to her Higher Power, she stopped burdening her friends with these concerns. Although she mentioned these problems to those who cared for her, her sharing was less intense and thus more bearable to her listeners. She no longer expected her friends and family members to fix these problems for her.

By relying on her Higher Power (and her many phone calls), Sandra found she could improve her communication skills in a wide variety of relationships. Praying before talking helped prevent her from blurting out whatever popped into her mind. She presented a more composed and professional image at work and became a more nurturing parent — all of which enhanced her self-esteem and lessened her need to eat.

Faith in her Higher Power also gave Sandra the courage to break off relationships that weren't in her best interest. She was willing to brave the loneliness, knowing that if she gave up bad relationships, her Higher Power would provide her with something better: an activity or a relationship that would build her self-esteem and help her grow.

Sandra has learned to place her recovery in her Higher Power's hands. She knows that she must follow the will of her Higher Power and be willing to do the necessary work. The speed of her weight loss, the depth of her self-understanding, and the rate of her spiritual progress are no longer under her control, but in the hands of her Higher Power. Each day she thanks her Higher Power for helping her continue on the path of recovery and for the relationships in her life. Deep inside herself, she now believes that her Higher Power wants her first and foremost to accept herself, and to go and live each day to the fullest extent possible.

Working the Steps

In O.A. we learn not to blame others for our disease, our frustrations with life, or other problems. Slowly, we let go of our blaming one day at a time, piece by piece, by practicing the Twelve Steps. This doesn't mean we deny or minimize the destructive or painful impact some persons have on our lives. The Twelve Step program of O.A. isn't a way of avoiding painful truths about others or ourselves. It's a way to confront these truths without being victimized by our emotions.

As we enter recovery, we learn to stop blaming ourselves for our disease. We may never know how or why we developed our problem with compulsive eating. But in O.A. we learn that the whys of our illness are unimportant compared to the hows: how we can recover, how we can fulfill and enjoy ourselves, how we can forgive ourselves and others, and how we can live life without being burdened by our food addiction, by our pasts, or by the imperfections in us and in others.

The Twelve Steps of Overeaters Anonymous

1. We admitted we were powerless over food — that our lives had become unmanageable.

2. Came to believe that a Power greater than ourselves could restore us to sanity.

3. Made a decision to turn our will and our lives over to the care of God *as we understood Him.*

4. Made a searching and fearless moral inventory of ourselves.

5. Admitted to God, to ourselves and to another human being the exact nature of our wrongs.

6. Were entirely ready to have God remove all these defects of character.

7. Humbly asked Him to remove our shortcomings.

8. Made a list of all persons we had harmed, and became willing to make amends to them all.

9. Made direct amends to such people wherever possible, except when to do so would injure them or others.

10. Continued to take personal inventory and when we were wrong, promptly admitted it.

11. Sought through prayer and meditation to improve our conscious contact with God *as we understood Him,* praying only for knowledge of His will for us and the power to carry it out.

12. Having had a spiritual awakening as the result of these steps, we tried to carry this message to compulsive overeaters and to practice these principles in all our affairs.*

The First Step teaches us that we are powerless over food. We can forgive ourselves for our illness. We aren't responsible for the fact that we are compulsive eaters, but we are responsible for our recovery.

In Step Two we learn that by admitting our powerlessness and relying on a Power greater than ourselves, we'll receive the strength to arrest our illness, one day at a time.

In Step Three, by turning our will and our lives over to God, we learn to trust that our Higher Power will take care of us, and that our future holds many possibilities other than compulsive eating.

While the Twelve Steps concern our relationship to food and to our Higher Power, the Steps also concern our relationships with others. In Steps Four to Ten we begin to acknowledge and accept our feelings in our relationships. As we

---

*Adapted from the Twelve Steps of Alcoholics Anonymous, reprinted with permission of A.A. World Services, Inc., New York, N.Y.

honestly examine our lives in Step Four, we may feel shame at realizing how our dishonesty, or some other character defect, has hurt others. Although Step Four asks us to take a moral inventory of ourselves, we may feel intense rage at realizing how we have been betrayed or viciously used by certain persons. Our shame or rage may overwhelm us.

Now that we have uncovered these powerful feelings, what do we do with them? The great temptation is to return to compulsive eating. Some of us find that the harder we work our program, the more we want to eat. This doesn't mean we aren't sincere about our recovery or that we're failures in O.A. Our increased desire to eat reflects, perhaps, our increased honesty in looking at ourselves and our relationships. Honest self-examination can cause pain and anxiety, and it's only normal for us to want to overeat when we're hurting, anxious, or confused.

But Steps Five, Six, Seven, and Eight give us an alternative to food: we can share our feelings with another person and our Higher Power (Step Five) and ask our Higher Power for help in dealing with our feelings and with our character defects (Steps Six and Seven). In Steps Eight and Nine, we try to make amends for the damage our negative emotions or character defects have caused. For example, we can write a letter, make a phone call, or talk in person to someone we've offended or cheated. We do this only if such action will not be harmful to someone else.

Amends are hardest to make to those who are dead or have moved far away. In such cases, we can write a letter to these people, or we can be kind to their loved ones. For instance, Rose made amends to her dead mother by volunteering two afternoons a week in a nursing home. While Rose began this as a duty, she came to enjoy her volunteer work and made it a part of her life.

Steps Eight and Nine can be tricky for those of us who tend to be people pleasers. We don't want to make a long list of every person we might have possibly harmed to even the slightest degree. Neither do we need to exhaust ourselves finding every person we've hurt, especially if they're scattered throughout the country. We shouldn't carry all the guilt for relationship problems in which the other person played a role.

Bert explains, "I've hurt several women in my life, but I'm not going to fly to Chicago to make an amend. Step Eight requires me to be willing to make amends, not to make every amend on my list.

"Actually I did have to track down the two women I hurt the most, but the rest of them, well, I'll wait until the situation presents itself. For example, if I'm in Chicago, I'll make a call or if that woman appears before me someday by chance, I'll apologize. Meanwhile, I'm working on changing myself so that I no longer hurt women like I used to."

Often, Steps Eight and Nine involve making amends to ourselves as well as others. Just as we may decide to stop lying in our relationships, we may also decide to limit our time with people who demoralize us, who are negative influences, or who push food on us. As part of our amends to ourselves, some of us have given ourselves gifts or taken vacations (even if we weren't yet at goal weight). Another amend we can make is to stop blaming ourselves for other people's moods and problems. If someone we love is unhappy, we might want to empathize and be supportive. But we don't have to make ourselves unhappy too. Neither do we have to help people with their problems unless we choose to. In making amends either to ourselves or to others, "keep it simple" is an important slogan to remember, for some of us can become obsessed with working the program.

In Step Ten we examine our lives frequently to see to what extent we've been motivated by fear, anger, doubt, or self-hate rather than by self-love, kindness, and gratitude. We may also look at the progress we've made in saying "no" to unnecessary requests and demands that threaten our abstinence. We can look at our progress in structuring our lives around some of our needs.

The beauty of O.A., or any Twelve Step program, is that it provides a path to self-awareness. A regular support group will support us as we uncover our buried feelings and confront our emotional difficulties. There are many friends to turn to as we work on and improve our relationships.

In addition, our O.A. friends and our Higher Power can help deal with some of our pain, anger, fear, and confusion. While their love and understanding don't make relationship problems disappear, their support can give us the courage to continue to be honest with ourselves. They can give us invaluable guidance and strength when we're trying to decide how to proceed in a relationship or whether to take any action at all.

In all the Steps, we develop and deepen our relationship with a Higher Power. As we work the Steps and get in touch with ourselves, there is great comfort in realizing that our Higher Power is always available to us.

A Healthy Recovery

Kay's Story

Recovery takes considerable effort. And just as recovery doesn't occur instantly after attending one meeting, relationships are not made smoother or more gratifying by one meaningful conversation or honest encounter. Often, taking more than one Fourth or Fifth Step on a particular relationship might be needed.

When Kay first came to O.A., she could barely talk about her feelings. While she found great relief in listening to others discuss their feelings, she couldn't identify any of her own. She couldn't distinguish anger from hurt, pain from guilt, or fear from shame. She was so depressed that the only emotions she had were anxiety and hopelessness. Her food compulsion was so out of control that at times she no longer wanted to live.

After getting a sponsor, Kay was able to identify her emotions more clearly. She saw anger behind her fears and anxieties and began a lengthy Fourth Step inventory. But she completed the Fourth Step, as she did many of the others, in an emotionally detached, intellectual manner. She produced a lengthy list of resentments toward her parents that she promptly turned over to her sponsor and her Higher Power. After asking her Higher Power to remove her resentments and making some amends, Kay thought she was finished.

But Kay had skipped a step, an important step, that of feeling her feelings. She had jumped from resentment to forgiveness without feeling any of her anger or hurt. She couldn't be truly healed of these strong feelings. Much of her eating, both in the past and in the present, could be called "revenge eating." Through food, she was trying to punish her father for his extra-marital affairs and her mother for her dependency on her daughter.

All during her teen years, when her father began to be increasingly absent from home, Kay's mother turned to Kay for support. Her mother almost turned Kay into a substitute husband and expected her to meet many emotional needs. Like an obedient daughter, Kay comforted her mother as much as possible and, when her father's affairs increased and her mother became too depressed to function, Kay did most of the housework and cared for her younger brothers and sisters.

Kay realized that she was missing out on dating and other fun. But she felt she had no choice but to help her mother. Meanwhile, she ate and ate and ate.

Kay finally left home, but she took her guilt, suppressed anger, food dependency, and shame with her. When she was well into the O.A. program, Kay knew in her mind that her parents weren't responsible for her compulsive eating, but, in her heart she blamed them almost entirely. *Why, if my father had been more of a father to me, I wouldn't have felt abandoned and unloved and had to turn to food for comfort,* she thought. *If my mother hadn't leaned on me all those years, surely I would have had a normal childhood and body size.*

Only when Kay had lost a noticeable amount of weight did her anger and hatred toward her parents emerge. These feelings, and guilt, led her to believe that if only she had been a better, more lovable daughter, her father would have spent more time at home. Kay felt like a failure because she had been unable to cure her mother of her depression. She had assumed responsibility for her parents' difficulties.

Recovery for Kay involved re-experiencing the pain of her parents' old arguments and feeling of helplessness. Recovery also involved periods of intense anger and hate, as well as periods of deep mourning for her lost youth. Sometimes Kay's feelings were so strong she could think of nothing else. She was afraid her feelings would kill her.

To live in the present, Kay found it necessary to complete yet another Fourth Step inventory on her parents and turn it over to her Higher Power. Only this time Kay realized that resolving her feelings toward her parents was more than a quick paper-and-pencil operation. She spent hours and hours writing about her feelings and sought professional help. At first, she believed she didn't deserve to be angry and resentful. After all, she hadn't been battered and her parents had provided for her material needs. Compared to others in O.A. who had suffered much worse, her pain, she believed, was trivial.

Kay learned not to trivialize her pain or to compare herself with others. She also learned that it was okay to be resentful and angry, but if she held on to these feelings they would destroy her. Not only would she eat when she had these feelings and gain weight, but she would be intensely troubled. Kay felt her Higher Power was always there to help lift the anger and pain, but she knew she also had to feel those feelings and share them with others before she could find serenity.

Kay was in O.A. for five years before she came to terms with her mother. Even today, she and her mother still have struggles. But at least today Kay realizes that she has choices. When her mother imposes on her for another favor, Kay's first choice is not to eat over her mother's request. Instead, she uses the O.A. tools to make her decisions.

By following the Steps, Kay now can say "no" to her mother without eating over the guilt of refusing her. Or she can say "yes" without eating over her resentment toward a mother who is rarely satisfied and highly critical.

Kay now can view her mother realistically. She can see her mother as a lonely woman whose manipulations were and are pleas for love and cries for help. "The more I forgive my mother, the thinner I get," says Kay. She takes each situation as it comes. Kay determines what she can or can't do for her mother. But she does not expect much thanks in return.

By working the Steps, Kay has learned to accept that her mother probably won't change. She has realized her powerlessness over her mother's personality and her mother's responses to her. Kay has given up her childhood role of trying to make her mother happy and earning her mother's approval. She has also had to surrender her wish to be mothered or parented by others, a wish that had clouded many of her relationships. Today, one day at a time, Kay is slowly learning to take care of, and approve of, herself.

Developing a Relationship with Ourselves

For many of us, life has been a continuous response to the needs, opinions, and emotions of others. Because we were — or are — overweight, we have found it hard to love and accept ourselves, even parts of ourselves unrelated to our body size. It has been easy for us to look for the approval, admiration, or love of others.

Yet we must now struggle to learn to love ourselves. Remember, self-love is a prerequisite for loving and relating meaningfully to others. Yet, many of us try to gain self-love by acquiring relationships, "purchasing" them if need be through monetary or other gifts, self-sacrifice, or other ways. Self-love is developed through self-knowledge, self-respect, and self-expression.

When we give up our love affair with food, we'll have increased time and energy for others, but we'll also need to take action for ourselves. The program promises that, one day at a time, we'll know what we need to do to be ourselves. For some of us, this will mean completing a project or developing a new talent. For others of us, it will mean making a new friend or discovering a new place to meditate and work the program.

At some point, we may be tempted to return to our food compulsion, or to become obsessed with money, sex, or relationships. All compulsions are ways we avoid taking responsibility for ourselves and avoid dealing with pain, grief, or other feelings.

After Susan lost weight in O.A., she spent two years obsessed with a relationship. Now she sees that her obsession with the relationship was a way to avoid grieving the death of her sister.

Paul, on the other hand, knew he had talent as a writer and wanted to write a novel about his childhood. But rather than take a writing course, he went on spending sprees and had relationships with two women. He now realizes that his new clothes and his relationships were ways of avoiding the risks and the work involved in pursuing his dream.

Conclusion

The Promises of Recovery for Relationships

Physical abstinence is the beginning of a new life, a new self. Only when we stop compulsively eating do we see how much our disease has affected every part of our life, including our relationships. Just as we are now better able to say "no" to excess food, we are also better able to exert some choice over our relationships.

When we were blinded by needs and fears due to bingeing, dieting, and the low self-esteem that resulted, we may have urgently sought to be with if not to cling to others rather than to honestly face our disease, our emotions, and our life problems. By immersing ourselves in others, we may have thought that we could obtain from them the love, approval, and direction which the program teaches us to slowly learn to obtain from ourselves and our Higher Power.

We are now in the position of exerting some degree of choice in our relationships. We may choose to end a relationship or change its course. Abstinence changes us not only physically, but also emotionally and spiritually. As we change, our relationships will also change. We will become more honest and communicate better. But this doesn't mean that others will always be open to our needs for intimacy and honesty. This realization can create more stress, possibly leading us back into the food. So we must work our program even harder and again remind ourselves that we're as powerless over others as we are over food.

While some might applaud our recovery, others might feel threatened by it. We'll probably need to talk more regularly with spouses, lovers, friends, or relatives who don't understand the new person we are becoming.

With abstinence, our relationships will also probably require more thought and prayer. By working the Steps we may decide to make positive changes in our relationships. Yet putting into practice even the simplest of changes isn't easy. Habits die hard. For example, we may want to stop criticizing our mate, or yelling at our children. At first, we may be successful in making such changes. But if these patterns are almost automatic, we may need help — we may need to turn to our O.A. friends and our Higher Power repeatedly for willingness and strength, and repeat Steps Six and Seven on certain relationship problems.

Understanding the motives behind our behavior can also be helpful. When we yell at a loved one, are we being judgmental and selfish, or is our criticism a cry for attention or love? When we get angry about the unswept floor, are we also indirectly saying, "I miss you. You don't seem to be spending much time with me anymore," or "Please pay attention to me and show me you love me." Similarly, when we share our vulnerabilities with persons who will not value our self-disclosure, are we talking compulsively, or are we asking for help or recognition?

Recovery promises us that if we stop eating compulsively, we'll be able to identify our true needs and desires in relationships. Further, we'll be given the self-love and the courage to ask that our needs be met in relationships. "This is a selfish program," we often hear. On the other hand, ours is also a program of service. Physical abstinence will eventually rid us of the self-absorption of compulsive eating or compulsive dieting. Self-seeking will slip away. The program promises us that we will lose interest in selfish things and gain interest in others.

"Before O.A., I never did anything for anyone else," states Kathy, an O.A. member. "All I thought about was my weight, how I looked, what others were going to think about my hips, my hair, my shoes, et cetera." She was also waiting to lose weight before she had relationships. Now Kathy is dating, and sponsoring an O.A. newcomer, despite being 50 pounds above her goal weight.

Recovery will also increase our understanding of others. With our heads clear of the destructive influence of too much food, we'll be able to perceive others more realistically and more positively. We'll feel less threatened by others and better able to accept them. We'll even be able to accept and love others without the assurance that they accept and love us in return.

The program also promises that as we learn more about ourselves, we'll love ourselves more. In addition, we'll be able to see how our experiences can help others who have faced similar problems. The program promises us we'll not regret the past nor wish to shut the door on it.

As we follow the O.A. recovery program, we're promised serenity and peace of mind, both in our relationships and in our solitude. When we're pierced by emotional pain in relationships, we'll have the courage to deal with the hurt, rather than to eat. Inside, we'll know that no matter how intense our suffering, our conflicts, or our fears, we'll not shatter.

In working the Twelve Steps and feeling confident that our Higher Power and our program friends are always there to help us, we'll be less afraid of relationships and their inevitable problems. Free of the need to be perfect and always right, we'll experience a new flexibility and spontaneity in all areas of life, including our relationships. The program promises us we'll intuitively know how to handle situations that once baffled us. We'll have ended our isolation.

The Twelve Steps of Alcoholics Anonymous*

1. We admitted we were powerless over alcohol — that our lives had become unmanageable.

2. Came to believe that a Power greater than ourselves could restore us to sanity.

3. Made a decision to turn our will and our lives over to the care of God *as we understood Him.*

4. Made a searching and fearless moral inventory of ourselves.

5. Admitted to God, to ourselves, and to another human being the exact nature of our wrongs.

6. Were entirely ready to have God remove all these defects of character.

7. Humbly asked God to remove our shortcomings.

8. Made a list of all persons we had harmed, and became willing to make amends to them all.

9. Made direct amends wherever possible, except when to do so would injure them or others.

10. Continued to take personal inventory and when we were wrong promptly admitted it.

11. Sought through prayer and meditation to improve our conscious contact with God *as we understood Him,* praying only for knowledge of His will for us and the power to carry that out.

12. Having had a spiritual awakening as the result of these steps, we tried to carry this message to alcoholics, and to practice these principles in all our affairs.

---

*The Twelve Steps are taken from *Alcoholics Anonymous* (Third Edition), published by A.A. World Services, Inc., New York, N.Y., pp. 59-60. Reprinted with permission.

BIBLIOGRAPHY

Erikson, Erik H. *Childhood and Society.* 2nd ed. New York: W. W. Norton & Co., 1950.

Fromm, Erich. *Escape from Freedom.* New York: Rinehart & Co., Inc., 1941.

Haley, Sarah. "I Feel a Little Sad: Applications of Object Relations Theory to the Hypnotherapy of Post-Traumatic Stress Disorders in Vietnam Veterans." Presentation at a conference of the Society for Clinical and Experimental Hypnosis, San Antonio, Texas, Oct. 25, 1984.

Hall, Calvin S. and Vernon J. Nordby. *A Primer of Jungian Psychology.* New York: Times-Mirror, 1973.

Kübler-Ross, Dr. Elisabeth. *Living with Death and Dying.* New York: Macmillan, 1982.

Moustakas, Clark E. *Loneliness.* Detroit: Prentice-Hall, Inc., 1961.

Tournier, Paul. *Four Best Books in One Volume: Guilt and Grace, The Meaning of Persons, The Person Reborn, To Understand Each Other.* New York: The Iverson Norman Association, 1977.

INDEX

Other titles that will interest you . . .

Fat Is a Family Affair
by Judi Hollis, Ph.D.
   A unique and moving discussion of eating disorders and the family's involvement, *Fat Is a Family Affair* has the honesty, frankness, and humor that could only come from someone who has been there. Part One, The Weigh In, tells how we became eating disorder sufferers, and Part Two, The Weigh Out, describes how we can start saying no to food and yes to life. 180 pp.
Order No. 1091

Keep Coming Back
Ongoing Support through O.A.
   For compulsive eaters, especially those with one or more years of solid recovery, *Keep Coming Back* explores the elements that comprise ongoing recovery from an eating disorder. It discusses the changes which come with long-term abstinence — how it can improve our relationships with other people, our social activities, our jobs and daily routines. 128 pp.
Order No. 5043

Listen to the Hunger
   Hunger can reflect a number of unsatisfied needs and can mask feelings of anger, fear, loneliness, fatigue, or boredom. One of your greatest resources is your inner voice that tells you who you are, what you feel, and what you need. *Listen to the Hunger* will teach you how to listen to the wisdom of that inner voice and discover what your hunger is all about. 71 pp.
Order No. 5008

For price and order information, please call one of our Customer Service Representatives.

HAZELDEN EDUCATIONAL MATERIALS

(800) 328-9000   **(800) 257-0070**   **(612) 257-4010**
(Toll Free. U.S. Only)   (Toll Free. MN Only)   (Alaska and Outside U.S.)
Pleasant Valley Road, Box 176, Center City, MN 55012- 0176